Evaluation for Inclusive and Sustainable Rural Transformation

Written by a team of expert practitioners at the Independent Office of Evaluation of IFAD, this book gives an overview of evaluation practice at IFAD.

It looks at how evaluation practice has evolved to reflect, respond to and inform changing expectations of development assistance. It reveals how evaluation products and methodologies have benefited from key reviews, revisions and lessons learned, and also how they have progressively strengthened IFAD's capacity to assess its operations and better understand its results. The book concludes with reflections on some of the challenges that lie ahead, including how the independent evaluation function can continue to evolve to meet future challenges and enhance the impact of development initiatives on people's lives.

This valuable insight into practice will be of interest to researchers, practitioners and policymakers in development economics, development studies and rural studies.

Oscar A. García is Director of the Independent Office of Evaluation of IFAD.

Osvaldo N. Feinstein is a member of the International Evaluation Advisory Panel of the United Nations Development Programme's Independent Evaluation Office and Professor at the Evaluation Master of Madrid Complutense University.

World Bank Series on Evaluation & Development

1. **Evaluation and Development**
   The Institutional Dimension
   Edited by Robert Picciotto and Eduardo Wiesner

2. **Involuntary Resettlement**
   Comparative Perspectives
   Edited by Robert Picciotto, Warren van Wicklin and Edward Rice

3. **Evaluation and Poverty Reduction**
   Edited by Osvaldo N. Feinstein and Robert Picciotto

4. **Making Development Work**
   Development Learning in a World of Poverty and Wealth
   Edited by Nagy Hanna and Robert Picciotto

5. **Managing a Global Resource**
   Challenges of Forest Conservation and Development
   Edited by Uma J. Lele

6. **Evaluation and Development**
   The Partnership Dimension
   Edited by Andres Liebenthal, Osvaldo N. Feinstein and Gregory K. Ingram

7. **Evaluating Development Effectiveness**
   Edited by Osvaldo N. Feinstein

8. **Evaluating Climate Change and Development**
   Edited by Rob D. van den Berg and Osvaldo N. Feinstein

9. **Evaluation for Inclusive and Sustainable Rural Transformation**
   Oscar A. García and Osvaldo N. Feinstein

For more information about this series, please visit: www.routledge.com/World-Bank-Series-on-Evaluation–Development/book-series/TRANWBSED

Evaluation for Inclusive and Sustainable Rural Transformation

World Bank Series on Evaluation and Development, Volume 9

Oscar A. García and Osvaldo N. Feinstein

Routledge
Taylor & Francis Group
LONDON AND NEW YORK

Independent Office of Evaluation
IFAD
Investing in rural people

First published 2019 by Routledge

2 Park Square, Milton Park, Abingdon, Oxfordshire OX14 4RN
52 Vanderbilt Avenue, New York, NY 10017

Routledge is an imprint of the Taylor & Francis Group, an informa business

First issued in paperback 2020

Library of Congress Cataloging-in-Publication Data
A catalog record for this title has been requested

ISBN: 978-1-138-60904-4 (hbk)
ISBN: 978-0-367-66607-1 (pbk)

Typeset in Bembo
by Sunrise Setting Ltd, Brixham, UK

Contents

List of Illustrations vii
List of Contributions viii
Foreword ix
Preface xi
Disclaimer xiii
Acknowledgements xiv
Abbreviations and Acronyms xv

1 **Introduction** 1

2 **Evolution of the Independent Evaluation Function at IFAD** 8

A. Key Phases 8
B. Key Structural Features 17
C. Evolving Methodology 20
D. IOE Evaluation Products 36

3 **Influential Evaluations** 53

A. Background 53
B. External Review of the Results and Impact of IFAD Operations (2002) 53
C. United Republic of Tanzania Country Portfolio Evaluation (2002/2003) 54
D. Independent External Evaluation of IFAD (2004/2005) 54
E. Corporate-Level Evaluations 55
F. African Development Bank (AfDB)–IFAD Joint Evaluation on Agriculture and Rural Development in Africa (2010) 66

4 Evaluations of Inclusive Development 69

A. Evaluation and Gender Mainstreaming 69
B. Evaluation and Indigenous Peoples 79
C. Evaluation and Pastoral Development 80
D. Evaluation of Rural Youth Interventions 82

5 Evaluations for Sustainable Development 85

A. Evaluation and Natural Resources Management 85
B. Evaluation and Environment Conservation in China 86
C. Evaluation and Water Conservation and Management 87

6 Learning and Knowledge Management 89

A. Focus Groups to Facilitate Learning and Monitoring 89
B. President's Report on the Implementation Status of Evaluation Recommendations and Management Actions (PRISMA) 89
C. Knowledge Management and the Philippines Country Strategy and Programme Evaluation 93

7 Partnerships in Evaluation 96

A. Evaluation Cooperation Group 96
B. Rome-Based Agencies Collaboration 96
C. United Nations Evaluation Group 97
D. Evaluation and Global or Regional Associations 97
E. Evaluation Partnership with Switzerland 98
F. Cooperation for Evaluation Capacity Development 98
G. Wilton Park 99

8 The Way Forward 100

A. Agenda 2030 and the Sustainable Development Goals 100
B. Evaluation and the Sustainable Development Goals 102
C. The Opportunities and Challenges of New Technologies 103
D. The Private Sector 107
E. Towards 2030 107

Appendix 1: Evaluation Methodology 110

Appendix 2: Evaluation Criteria, Key Questions and Ratings 133

Index 143

Illustrations

Chart

4.1 Number of GEWE practices in the sample classed by categories and areas 75

Figures

2.1 Key milestones and evaluations in the evolution of IOE 18
2.2 Theoretical map of the correspondence between COSOP objectives and lending and non-lending activities 44
3.1 Scheme of the typical process of evaluations at institutional level 55
3.2 Notional results chain for IFAD's engagement with fragile states 62
4.1 Main elements of policy on gender equality and women's empowerment 70
6.1 Outline of key interactions with partners in an evaluation process. 90

Tables

2.1 Main modifications between the first and second editions of the Evaluation Manual 22
2.2 Definition and rating of the evaluation criteria used by IOE 25
A1.1 The most frequently used data collection methods 116
A2.1 Rating system 140
A2.2 Score descriptors 141

Contributions (in order of appearance)

First Phases of the Evaluation Function at IFAD
Osvaldo Feinstein

The Importance of an Independent Evaluation Function
Luciano Lavizzari

Reflections on the Journey of the Office of Evaluation from a Studies-Oriented Unit to a Fully-Fledged Independent Outfit
Mona Bishay

IFAD's Evaluation Committee: Focusing on What Works, What Does Not Work, and How IFAD Can Better Serve People Living in Rural Poverty
Margot Skarpeteig

The Harmonization Agreement between Independent Evaluation and Self-Evaluation in IFAD
Ashwani K. Muthoo

Innovating through Evaluation Work
Paolo Silveri

IOE's First Impact Evaluation
Fabrizio Felloni

Country Programme Evaluations
Khalid El Harizi

Do Empowered Rural Women Organizations in Nepal and Papua New Guinea Address Child Undernutrition?
Per Eklund

PRISMA Closes the Learning Loop
Caroline Heider

Foreword

Over the years, independent evaluation has helped increase the impact of IFAD's operations for sustainable and inclusive rural transformation. The Fund's evaluation function has evolved over many years, beginning with an internal monitoring and evaluation unit within IFAD. The creation in 2003 of a fully-fledged independent office reporting directly to the Executive Board was a major milestone. It brought IFAD into line with the practice of other international financial institutions. Since then, the role of the Independent Office of Evaluation (IOE) has become increasingly robust as it strives to ensure accountability, learning and transparency.

Independent evaluation has been found to be critically important to development. In the case of IFAD, the way the Fund operates reflects the key insights and findings presented in independent evaluations, and the implementation of evaluation recommendations by IFAD and its partners in development in their activities. For example, one of the first influential evaluations was the Tanzania Country Portfolio Evaluation in 2002–2003, which highlighted the need for IFAD to establish a more permanent country presence. Today, IFAD has 40 country offices worldwide.

Perhaps most significantly, the Independent External Evaluation of IFAD undertaken between 2004 and 2005 resulted in an action plan to enhance IFAD's development effectiveness that led to the move to direct supervision of projects, and a wide range of important structural and organizational changes, new corporate policies, and the streamlining of internal processes and procedures. All of these actions have made IFAD a stronger organization, better able to deliver development results and value for money.

The annual corporate-level evaluations of IFAD's policies, strategies, business processes and organizational aspects provide an ongoing source of ideas on how to make IFAD work better and deliver more. They have resulted in tangible operational changes related to such areas as direct supervision, field presence, efficiency, gender, natural resource management, rural finance, working in fragile situations, and the Performance-based Allocation System, to name a few.

As IFAD grows and changes to maximize its impact on the Sustainable Development Goals, the independent evaluation function will continue to be an indispensable tool. Its methodological rigour and focus on learning and accountability should enable IFAD to further develop better instruments and policies to pursue its goals of promoting rural transformation and strengthening its investment in rural people.

Gilbert F. Houngbo
President of the International Fund for Agricultural Development (IFAD)

Preface

Better results, better lives. This, in short, is the vision that has inspired the work of IFAD and, hence, the ongoing evolution of independent evaluation of the Fund's efforts. Independent evaluation has come to be recognized as a powerful instrument to enhance the effectiveness of international development efforts in support of sustainable and inclusive rural transformation, especially in the context of the 2030 sustainable development agenda.

The Independent Office of Evaluation of IFAD (IOE) aims to promote accountability and learning through independent, credible and useful evaluations, in keeping with its mandate. IOE evaluates IFAD-funded projects and programmes, provides assessments of what works and what does not, identifies the factors leading to good performance, and determines to what extent IFAD's policies and strategies are successful in tackling poverty alleviation in rural areas. More importantly, evaluation should be able to respond to the 'why?' question. Applying internationally recognized principles, norms and standards, IOE uses its analytical rigour to understand the context, conditions and factors that lead to changes in development situations under IFAD-financed operations.

IOE conducts its work with an eye to increasing the impact of IFAD's work, spurring innovation in evaluation methodologies, and stimulating learning, growth and dynamic partnerships. There is much to be learned from an overview of evaluation at IFAD, which has evolved over the years to offer new and better ways to assess the impact and accountability of development projects, programmes and policies.

Between 1983 and 2015, IOE conducted more than 400 evaluations at the country, corporate, thematic and project levels. In that time, evaluation at IFAD has gone from being a management support function to a fully-fledged independent evaluation outfit, with a direct reporting line to the Fund's Executive Board.

In the years to come, evaluation practice will need to keep pace with changing conditions and new challenges in order to meet the increasing global demand for credible, useful and quick results in development. There have been dramatic shifts in the ways in which countries achieve economic growth while striving to protect limited natural resources. Private sector and market-oriented development initiatives have gained prominence in the development arena, as has recognition of the importance of engaging community-based organizations.

Successful action in the future will require flexible, adaptive and proactive institutions that can make use of the knowledge and information gained through evaluation. As Director of IFAD's Independent Office of Evaluation, I am pleased to say that the evaluation function at IFAD has contributed significantly to improving the Fund's policies and strategies. I appreciate the Fund's solid commitment to further improving its operations by understanding the results and impact of its work through the evaluation process.

This publication offers an overview of how the mission and methodologies of independent evaluation at IFAD have evolved. It shows how evidence-gathering has grown to better inform and engage development actors, including those in government and in rural communities. Additionally, it offers informative examples of influential evaluations and highlights from IOE's Evaluation Manual. This book also offers reflections on how the independent evaluation function can continue to evolve to meet future challenges and enhance the impact of development initiatives on people's lives.

Oscar A. García
Director
Independent Office of Evaluation of IFAD

Disclaimer

The Independent Office of Evaluation of IFAD (IOE) conducts evaluations of IFAD-financed policies, strategies and operations to promote accountability and learning. The main purpose is to contribute to improving IFAD's and its partners' performance in reducing rural poverty in recipient countries. IOE's independent evaluations assess the impact of IFAD-funded activities and give an analysis of successes and shortcomings – to tell it the way it is – as well as identify factors affecting performance. Based on the key insights and recommendations drawn from evaluation findings, IOE also shares IFAD's knowledge and experience in agriculture and rural development with a wider audience.

The views expressed in this publication do not necessarily reflect those of IFAD's Member States or their representatives to its Executive Board. The designations employed and the presentation of material in this publication do not imply the expression of any opinion whatsoever on the part of IFAD concerning the legal status of any country, territory, city or area or of its authorities, or concerning the delimitation of its frontiers or boundaries. The designations 'developed' and 'developing' countries are intended for statistical convenience and do not necessarily express a judgement about the stage reached by a particular country or area in the development process.

Acknowledgements

This publication was prepared by Osvaldo Feinstein, Professor in the Evaluation Master's Programme of the Complutense University of Madrid, and Oscar A. García, Director of the Independent Office of Evaluation of IFAD (IOE). They were ably supported by Charmaine Wilkerson, IOE consultant, who contributed to writing the first draft, and Melba E. Alvarez-Pagella, former IOE Evaluation Communication and Knowledge Management Officer, who coordinated the production and contributed to the revision. Brett Shapiro, IOE consultant, edited a preliminary version of the document.

Special thanks are extended to Mona Bishay, Per Eklund, Khalid El Harizi, Fabrizio Felloni, Caroline Heider, Luciano Lavizzari, Ashwani K. Muthoo and Margot Skarpeteig for sharing their valuable experiences related to IOE's work and evolution.

Abbreviations and Acronyms

ACP	Agreement at Completion Point
AfDB	African Development Bank
ARRI	Annual Report on Results and Impact of IFAD Operations
CBO	community-based organization
CLE	corporate-level evaluation
CLEE	Corporate-Level Evaluation on IFAD's Efficiency
COSOP	country strategic opportunities programme
CPE	country programme evaluation
CSPE	country strategy and programme evaluation
ECG	Evaluation Cooperation Group (of multilateral development banks)
ECU	Evaluation Communication Unit
ENRM	environmental and natural resources management
FAO	Food and Agriculture Organization of the United Nations
GEWE	Gender equality and women's empowerment
ICT	information and communications technology
IEE	Independent External Evaluation
IFI	international financial institution
IOE	Independent Office of Evaluation of IFAD
JES	joint evaluation synthesis
LAC	Latin America and the Caribbean
M&E	monitoring and evaluation
MDGs	Millennium Development Goals
MIC	middle-income country
NEP	new evaluation processes
OE	Office of Evaluation; Office of Evaluation and Studies
OECD/DAC	Organisation for Economic Co-operation and Development/Development Assistance Committee
PBAS	performance-based allocation system
PCR	project completion report
PCRV	project completion report validation
PMD	Programme Management Department
PNG	Papua New Guinea

PPE	project performance evaluation
PRISMA	President's Report on the Implementation Status of Evaluation Recommendations and Management Actions
RMF	Results Management Framework
SDG	Sustainable Development Goal
SKD	Strategy and Knowledge Department
UNEG	United Nations Evaluation Group
WFP	World Food Programme

1 Introduction

An estimated 3.4 billion people live in rural areas in the world today. Two-thirds of these rural inhabitants depend on roughly 500 million small and family farms for their livelihoods. Rural development can have a direct and positive impact on the incomes and food and nutrition security of rural populations. It also affects quality of life through improved education, healthcare and other critical services. In other words, rural development remains one of the most effective ways to overcome poverty.

In September 2015, United Nations Member States formally adopted the 2030 Agenda, which aims to 'leave no one behind' in achieving the Sustainable Development Goals (SDGs). The 17 SDGs, along with their 169 targets, form a comprehensive list which spans social, environmental, economic and governance issues and which, throughout, acknowledge the pivotal role that rural development plays in this collective effort to 'transform our world' as envisioned by the 2030 Agenda. It was about time for such a vision of sustainable development to take centre stage in the international agenda. A holistic vision that puts people at the centre and realizes that we must take into account the environment and the capacity of the planet to host us. A holistic vision that recognizes that prosperity and economic development are necessary for all the inhabitants of the planet, and not only for the better-off. Furthermore, the 2030 Agenda offers the world an action plan that tackles head-on the challenges of increasing inequality. It is an agenda that understands that no matter how big our country or organization may be, we need to work together, in partnerships, to achieve a secure and brighter future for our children and future generations. The new sustainable development agenda is a call for action and a call for transformative change. Together with the SDGs, it revolves around 'People, Planet, Prosperity, Peace and Partnerships'.[1] The recognition, in the SDGs, of the importance of rural areas and agriculture ties directly into the International Fund for Agricultural Development's (IFAD) mandate (International Fund for Agricultural Development website, n.d.).

Evaluation has a vital role to play in the international development community and, ultimately, in efforts to improve lives. In recent years, the international development community has increased its focus on measuring and improving, more comprehensively and holistically, the results of its work. This publication shares elements of IFAD's long experience in this regard, especially in light of the

Fund's focus on investing in rural and agricultural transformation, and its unique role in achieving the SDGs.

This book has been produced by the Independent Office of Evaluation (IOE) of IFAD (Independent Office of Evaluation of IFAD website, n.d.) to provide an overview of evaluation practice at IFAD and how its evolution reflects, responds to and informs changing expectations of development assistance. It shares information on how evaluation products and methodologies have benefited from key reviews, revisions and lessons learned, and also how they have progressively strengthened IFAD's capacity to assess its operations and better understand its results. Additionally, in the concluding section 'The Way Forward', this book offers reflections on some of the challenges that lie ahead. First, we take a closer look at IFAD's mandate and the ways in which the evaluation function has evolved to date.

About IFAD

IFAD was established in 1977 as a unique specialized agency of the United Nations, and also an international financial institution (IFI). IFAD is the only IFI with a specific mandate to reduce rural poverty through investments in agriculture and rural development. IFAD invests in rural people for economic, social and cultural impact in support of sustainable and inclusive rural transformation. It aims to empower people to reduce poverty, increase food security, improve nutrition and strengthen resilience.

The decision to form the Fund was one of the major outcomes of the 1974 World Food Conference. One of the most important insights emerging from that conference was the recognition that the causes of food insecurity and famine were not so much failures in food production as they were structural problems relating to poverty, and to the fact that the majority of the developing world's poor populations were concentrated in rural areas. This remains true, despite dramatic changes in international dynamics and impressive gains in reducing poverty and hunger over the years.

IFAD is the leading multilateral investor in the livelihoods of poor rural producers in developing countries worldwide. Since 1978, IFAD has provided US$18.9 billion in grants and low-interest loans to projects that support agricultural and rural development and have reached about 470 million people. The Fund's initiatives target women and men smallholder farmers, landless workers, artisanal fishers, nomadic pastoralists, forest communities and indigenous peoples, helping them to increase food production, raise incomes and improve livelihoods, while sustainably managing natural resources and adapting to climate change. IFAD is dedicated to eradicating rural poverty in developing countries.

By raising productivity, the programmes and projects funded by IFAD make it possible for smallholders to move beyond subsistence farming and grow surplus produce for the market. IFAD supports training and capacity-building and cooperates with local communities to help them organize themselves and strengthen their institutions.

Working with poor rural people, governments, donors, non-governmental organizations and many other partners, IFAD focuses on country-specific solutions, which can involve increasing poor rural people's access to financial services, markets, technology, land and other natural resources, and improving infrastructure. The projects supported by the organization are often in remote and environmentally fragile locations and with marginalized and disenfranchised populations. It is of particular importance to the Fund's mission to focus attention on the challenges faced by women, the young and indigenous peoples.

IFAD has a wealth of expertise in areas which greatly influence the lives of poor rural people, particularly those who depend on agriculture for their livelihood, including smallholders in remote rural communities. It champions effective innovations in smallholder agriculture and rural poverty reduction, and promotes their replication and scaling up. The unique characteristics of IFAD's approach to agriculture and rural development include:

- an emphasis on smallholder farmers and producers as businesses
- a focus on empowering rural women and supporting the many roles they play in agriculture
- the ability to bring together individuals and organizations from diverse sectors
- support for country leadership on development, based on the mutual trust and confidence of our borrowing Member States, and built up over many years
- expertise in targeting resources to those who are most in need and who have the potential to be economically productive
- a focus on capacity-building and empowerment of communities and organizations of poor rural producers.

As of May 2017, there are 40 IFAD country offices worldwide. Having a permanent presence in-country enables the organization to design programmes and projects more precisely and supervise them more closely, while also reducing response times and decreasing costs. In addition, country presence makes it easier for IFAD to work with government officials, locally hired staff and civil society organizations, thus building skills and knowledge in the country. Other benefits of a stable presence on the ground include more effective engagement in country-level policy dialogue, better alignment of programmes with national policies, more robust national ownership and leadership of programmes, and stronger partnerships with other donors. Where it has a local presence, IFAD is a member of the United Nations country team and participates in developing and implementing the United Nations Development Assistance Framework, contributing to an efficient team approach to achieving the SDGs.

Governance. The **Governing Council**[2] is IFAD's highest decision-making authority. Each Member State is represented in the Governing Council by Governors, Alternate Governors and other designated advisers. IFAD has an **Executive Board**[3] **comprised of 36 Member States, which** is responsible for overseeing the general operations of IFAD and for approving its programme of work.

Membership of the Executive Board is determined by the Governing Council and is allocated among countries from the Organisation for Economic

Co-operation and Development (OECD), the Organization of the Petroleum Exporting Countries, and other countries from the three regional subdivisions of developing countries among IFAD's Member States.

United Nations partners. There are three food and agriculture organizations of the United Nations headquartered in Rome: the Food and Agriculture Organization of the United Nations (FAO), IFAD and the World Food Programme (WFP). The agencies have different but complementary mandates, and collaborate on an ongoing basis.

As a fund, IFAD's role is to mobilize resources to invest in development opportunities for poor rural people. The Fund works in close collaboration with borrowing-country governments and local communities to design, supervise and assess country-led programmes and projects that support smallholders and poor rural producers. FAO works with member countries to develop global norms and the sharing of information, analyses and knowledge on agriculture, while also providing policy and technical assistance. WFP is primarily the food-aid arm of the United Nations system, with an extensive global field presence and logistical and procurement capacities.

The agencies frequently work together, and most intensively at country level, to pool expertise and comparative advantage.

Loans to Member States. Like many other development finance institutions, IFAD uses a performance-based allocation system (PBAS) to allocate loans to Member States. The system also covers the allocations of country grant resources, including grants under the debt sustainability framework. The IFAD PBAS allocates resources on the basis of rural population, per capita gross national income and country performance. Country performance includes the broad policy framework, rural development policy and the performance of the IFAD-supported portfolio.

The PBAS aims to ensure that resources are allocated to the countries where need is greatest and the funds will produce real results on the ground. While such systems support strong performers, they also take into account the important needs of borrowing countries that, despite poor performance, require assistance. Other institutions which use the PBAS approach to provide loans on a concessional basis include the African Development Bank, the Asian Development Bank, the Caribbean Development Bank, the Global Environment Facility, the Inter-American Development Bank and the International Development Association of the World Bank. They implement a system that assesses both performance and need, and IFAD meets with them annually to review issues and progress.

IFAD Management revised the design of the PBAS as a result of the corporate-level evaluation of the PBAS conducted by IOE in 2015/2016.[4] The evaluation (International Fund for Agricultural Development, 2016) pointed out areas for further improvement around two main topics: the formula and the PBAS management process. In particular, IFAD Management has followed up on the evaluation recommendations related to: (I) streamlining the PBAS process for better effectiveness; (ii) improving efficiency; (iii) improving management and governance; and (iv) generating learning. Additionally, a number of improvements have been added to the allocation formula, which now incorporates indicators that approximate welfare conditions of the rural poor in the areas served by IFAD.

IFAD's financing is drawn from several sources: initial capital, investment income, loan reflows and contributions from Member States and multilateral institutions. These contributions come through regular replenishments and in the form of supplementary funds.

Challenges to Rural Development

It is estimated that nearly 70 per cent of the world's population will be living in urban areas by 2050. Still, it is important to recognize that urban and rural areas have a symbiotic relationship. Going forward, they will need each other to survive. Rural areas around the world lag behind urban areas on virtually all development indicators, and large numbers of rural youth faced with dismal prospects are looking off the farm for future opportunities.

In this context, IFAD and its partners in development will need to be flexible and adapt to new information and ideas, in order to meet new challenges. The global economy has experienced major structural shifts, with the emergence of greater private sector investment in development, stronger markets in middle-income economies, rising urbanization and a growing demand for food, and with some of the world's fastest growth rates taking place in several low-income developing countries.

Other influences that come into play include shocks brought on by climate change, erratic energy prices and complex and protracted conflicts. Several regions have seen large-scale population displacements within and across national borders, and the social and political upheavals linked to unemployment are deepening. Despite impressive reductions in poverty globally, progress has been uneven, and economic inequality across the developed and developing worlds alike is increasing. It should be noted that three-quarters of the world's extremely poor people now live in middle-income countries (MICs).

The Role of Evaluation

Independent evaluations help to capture lessons learned and identify areas for greater effectiveness and impact.

> *Systematic independent evaluation of completed projects and past and ongoing policies and strategies is indispensable if IFAD is to learn from its experience, both positive and negative, and improve its future effectiveness.* Revised IFAD Evaluation Policy (International Fund for Agricultural Development 2011).

The evaluation function has played an important role in the work of IFAD since the Fund began activities in 1978. What began as the Monitoring and Evaluation Unit later changed its name, reporting lines, and operational and organizational characteristics, to become the Independent Office of Evaluation, a fully independent outfit reporting directly to the Fund's Executive Board.

Over the years, IFAD Management has made use of the information and insights produced by evaluations, with impact being seen in corporate policies and country programme levels. Evaluation has become a potent mechanism for change in IFAD, leading to numerous reforms and significant institutional changes that have helped the Fund improve its institutional and operational effectiveness, and develop better instruments and policies to enable the rural poor to empower themselves to overcome their poverty.

IOE at a Glance

IOE conducts evaluations of IFAD-financed policies, strategies and operations to promote accountability and learning, with a view to improving the performance of IFAD and its partners. IOE has developed a common strategic, medium-term vision for 2016–2025 to guide decisions on IOE's undertakings, work programme and budget.

Mission

Promote accountability and learning through independent, credible and useful evaluations of IFAD's work.

Vision

Increase the impact of IFAD's operations for sustainable and inclusive rural transformation through excellence in evaluation.

Strategies

1 Building a stronger impact-oriented culture in IFAD
2 Bringing innovation to evaluation methodologies
3 Stimulating learning and growth in all our engagements
4 Creating dynamic partnerships
5 Developing and empowering our staff
6 Giving voice to the voiceless

Notes

1 www.sustainabledevelopment.un.org/post2015/transformingourworld.
2 www.ifad.org/who/governance/tags/gc/2082356.
3 www.ifad.org/who/governance/tags/eb/2082318.
4 www.ifad.org/evaluation/reports/cle/tags/pba/y2016/20995915.

References

Independent Office of Evaluation of IFAD website: www.ifad.org/evaluation.

International Fund for Agricultural Development website: www.ifad.org.

International Fund for Agricultural Development. 2011. Evaluation Policy. Independent Office of Evaluation of IFAD. Rome: IFAD.

International Fund for Agricultural Development. 2016. IFAD's Performance-Based Allocation System Corporate-level Evaluation. Independent Office of Evaluation of IFAD. Rome: IFAD.

2 Evolution of the Independent Evaluation Function at IFAD

A. Key Phases

The Early Years

From the very beginning, IFAD's Member States, governing bodies and management recognized that the strength of IFAD's future performance would benefit from an understanding of the results and impact of its activities through evaluation. However, the origins of the evaluation function at IFAD were markedly different from its current form as an independent outfit.

Soon after being established in 1978, IFAD Management set up an internal evaluation function, but this role was combined with monitoring as part of IFAD's Monitoring and Evaluation Unit. The Unit reported to the Assistant President of what was then the Economic and Planning Department, and was headed by a unit chief. Its focus was primarily on mid-term evaluations during project implementation.

Early on, the Unit did not conduct full-scale evaluations, since IFAD-supported projects were in their early stages. In 1982, the Unit was transformed into the Monitoring and Evaluation Division, reporting to the Assistant President of the Economic Policy Department.

In 1988, a study reviewed the monitoring and evaluation (M&E) experience of IFAD in all regions and recommended that the two functions – monitoring and evaluation – be separated. By then, an extensive debate had been taking place among development organizations on the value of independent evaluation.

First Phases of the Evaluation Function at IFAD

By Osvaldo Feinstein, former IOE Senior Evaluation Officer (from 1989 to 1997) and IOE consultant since 1982.

During its first years of existence, IFAD was committed to developing a fully-fledged M&E function. The M&E Division's main activity was to develop an M&E function within IFAD-assisted projects by establishing dedicated M&E units. During its initial years, the division played two roles: (1) contributing to the design of the M&E units at project level, based on demands from the regional divisions; and (2) developing M&E guidelines for the design of the units. In this second area, the division produced manuals and guidelines on M&E for agricultural development projects. These publications have been useful not only for IFAD but for the development community at large.

In 1988, during the interim period between the first two directors (Ram Malhotra until 1987 and Pierre Spitz since May 1989), a study was conducted on IFAD's M&E experience in all the regions. Two key conclusions of that study were that the M&E units were not functioning well; and that the M&E design at project level had a fundamental inconsistency: monitoring was meant to be linked to project management, whereas the evaluation function had to be independent from project management. Therefore, the project-level M&E units had an inconsistent mandate: they had to work very closely with project management, but at the same time they had to be independent. The study found that a few M&E units performed well in the monitoring function but failed on the evaluation side, whereas another set of units performed well in the evaluation function, but failed on monitoring. A key recommendation was that the two functions – monitoring and evaluation – be separated, with different budget lines.

That study also pointed out that there was an evaluation capacity constraint. It therefore recommended that evaluation capacity be developed. As a consequence, IFAD's Office of Evaluation and Studies (as the M&E division was renamed in 1994) designed a technical assistance grant, Programme for Strengthening the Regional Capacity for Evaluation of Rural Poverty Alleviation Projects in Latin America and the Caribbean (PREVAL), approved in 1997, to enhance evaluation capacities in Latin America and the Caribbean region. PREVAL was partly replicated in Africa, and was the first programme in the world fully dedicated to evaluation capacity-building.

M&E at IFAD was launched more than 30 years ago, and the Fund was a world pioneer in this area. When IFAD started conducting evaluation missions, stakeholders (government, beneficiaries, management, etc.) were not very keen on being evaluated. The whole development community did not fully realize the potential of such a tool. The situation today has changed remarkably, and IFAD has played a pivotal role in increasing the awareness of the importance of evaluation and promoting the strengthening of evaluation capacities.

Rapid External Assessment (1994)[1]

In 1994, a Rapid External Assessment of IFAD (Attiga, 1994) was undertaken during the negotiations of the Fourth Replenishment of IFAD's Resources. One of the recommendations put forward in the assessment was that the evaluation function be separated from monitoring. This led to the establishment of the Office of Evaluation and Studies (OE), which was independent of operations and incorporated into the Office of the President. By then, the staff had grown and was headed by a director.

The assessment also identified some positive trends resulting from evaluation which had contributed to IFAD's widely recognized intellectual leadership. It noted, for example, that the Fund's evaluation function had contributed new thinking on participatory approaches in evaluating rural poverty and related environmental issues. However, it also reported a lack of capacity for follow-up action, and made the following suggestions:

- A more active programme of thematic studies, based on the growing stock of project evaluations and, in due course, of country portfolio evaluations;
- Increased dissemination to external audiences;
- More attention to the impact of evaluation experience on policy, formulating guidelines and operations; and
- Learning more systematically from the evaluation experience of others, including bilateral donors.

New Approach to Evaluation and New Evaluation Processes

In 1999, OE formulated a new approach to evaluation aimed at improving performance and grounded in opportunities to generate concrete solutions and knowledge for use both by its partners and by development practitioners. To drive learning towards action, it introduced three main features to the new evaluation processes (NEP), which to date continue to be practised:

- The **Approach Paper** as the starting point of each evaluation. One of the most important features of this process is the agreement from the outset, which brings the main actors together to identify and agree upon the key issues to be analysed. This results-oriented approach assures that the NEP will respond to the needs of the partnership. It improves the quality of evaluation design, since it establishes the appropriate methodological approach based on a preliminary evaluability study.
- The concept of the **core learning partnership** to steer the evaluation process throughout its cycle. The core learning partnership is an informal and flexible platform to build ownership and open deliberations among the key partners in the evaluation process. It serves as an effective and real-time transfer of knowledge and learning generated through evaluation to design and operation.
- The definition of the **completion point** of each evaluation process as an agreement or understanding among IOE and its partners, now known as the **Agreement at Completion Point** (ACP). At this step, the learning and knowledge generated by the evaluation are officially acknowledged and internalized within IFAD's knowledge systems and by the partnership. The written agreement or understanding illustrates the stakeholders'

consensus and commitment to implement, and take follow-up actions on, evaluation recommendations which are expected to improve project operations, policies or future project design. The ACP is now particularly relevant for country strategy and programme evaluations.[2]

Towards an Independent Evaluation Function

The 2002 Consultation on the Sixth Replenishment of IFAD's Resources urged IFAD Management to create an independent evaluation function. In accordance with the Evaluation Policy approved in 2003, the Office of Evaluation and Studies became independent of IFAD Management in the evaluations it was to conduct.

The name was changed to the Office of Evaluation, and the director of the division would directly and exclusively report to IFAD's Executive Board, which has overseen independent evaluations since then. This landmark decision made IFAD the first United Nations agency, programme and fund with an independent office of evaluation.

The Importance of an Independent Evaluation Function

Luciano Lavizzari, former IOE Director (1999 to 2012)

The independence of the evaluation function, so important to the role of IOE today, was not on the agenda when IFAD was established in the late 1970s. Originally, the evaluation function was contained in IFAD's Monitoring and Evaluation Unit. Later, it became a division reporting to the Assistant President, Economic Policy Department and, still later, the Office of Evaluation and Studies, with its director reporting directly to the President of IFAD.

Another important change, in 1987, led to the establishment of the Evaluation Committee as a subsidiary body of IFAD's Executive Board. The Committee was given the mandate to assist the Executive Board by undertaking in-depth reviews of evaluations and studies, and its function and rules of procedure have since been added to and refined.

After 1996, the concept of evaluation independence was the subject of debate among IFIs (international financial institutions). Most IFIs established their own independent evaluation offices and subsequently removed the oversight function of management over those offices. At IFAD, the 2002 Consultation on the Sixth Replenishment of IFAD's Resources urged management to create an independent evaluation function. The rationale given for this proposal was that such independence would contribute to an objective process that could sustain the confidence of member countries over the long run and help realize the full value of the evaluation function at IFAD.

Why this debate over the importance of independent evaluation? It is widely acknowledged that political power tends to become corruptive and distorting in the absence of concrete mechanisms for checks and balances. The management of development agencies is no exception to this rule. The executive boards provide oversight on major policy issues, but their oversight rarely extends to the details of operations, including their achievements and failures. The basic rationale for an independent evaluation and an independent evaluation office is, therefore, the need for an institutional arrangement, independent from management, that 'speaks the truth' about results and failures to governing bodies, member countries and, eventually, their taxpayers.

The existence of an independent evaluation office which, in effect, looks over management's shoulders, also helps managers to be more realistic and objective in their assessment and reporting. Independence is now widely recognized as one of the key evaluation principles. In fact, the other principles – credibility, usefulness and transparency – depend directly or indirectly on the extent to which an evaluation is independent.

IFAD's Evaluation Policy was approved by the Executive Board in April 2003, and was revised in 2011. The original Policy contained a number of arrangements concerning the reporting body for IOE, the independence of the IOE director and staff, and the control over the work programme and budget, in addition to IOE's independence in reporting and disclosing evaluation reports. These arrangements largely coincided with the Good Practice Standards on Independence which were approved by the Evaluation Cooperation Group (ECG) in 2010 (Evaluation Cooperation Group, 2010), the same year in which the ECG conducted a Peer Review of IFAD's evaluation function. OE was renamed and became the Independent Office of Evaluation.

While the underpinnings of the original Policy remain valid to this day, the revised Policy incorporated important clarifications and the recommendations of the Peer Review. It also updated the Policy in light of changes that had taken place at IFAD and in its evaluation function since 2003. These include the approval of the Fund's Direct Supervision and Implementation Support Policy, the introduction of IFAD country presence, and further development of the self-evaluation system. The focus of the revised document is mainly on evaluation, which at IFAD is performed independently on behalf of the Executive Board. It also covers essential aspects of IFAD Management's self-evaluation system, especially those areas which directly affect IOE's independent evaluation work. The document, divided into three parts, covers the policy framework, evaluation principles, operational policies, organizational measures and other key points.

First Evaluation Policy (2003)

IFAD's first Evaluation Policy (2003) aimed at strengthening both accountability and learning for better development results on the ground and paved the way for an independent evaluation function to be introduced.

Independence of IFAD's Evaluation Function: Key Provisions in the Evaluation Policy

- The Director reports to the Executive Board rather than to the IFAD President.
- The work programme and budget are prepared independently of IFAD Management and presented directly to the Executive Board and Governing Council for approval.
- The President delegates his authority to make all human resource decisions related to the [Independent] Office of Evaluation to its Director.
- The Director is appointed for one non-renewable term of six years.

The Director is authorized to issue evaluation reports to IFAD Management, the Fund's governing bodies and the public at large without seeking the clearance of any official outside of IOE.

ECG's Peer Review of IFAD's Office of Evaluation and Evaluation Function

In 2009/2010, the ECG conducted a peer review of IFAD's Office of Evaluation and evaluation function,[3] the first ever by the ECG. The review was required in order for IOE to be accepted as a fully-fledged member in 2010. It covered the Office of Evaluation, the IFAD Evaluation Policy, management's self-evaluation system and the oversight function of the Evaluation Committee. Acceptance of IOE into the ECG played an important role in the evolution of the evaluation function at IFAD.

The ECG found that the Evaluation Policy provided a sound framework for an effective, independent evaluation function and that a number of evaluation products, such as the Independent External Evaluation of IFAD and corporate-level evaluations – such as the direct supervision, country presence and rural finance evaluations – had had strategic impact at the corporate level. The ECG further cited the country programme evaluations (CPEs) and the Annual Report on Results and Impact (ARRI) as being widely viewed as useful products.

The review made a series of recommendations for IOE that further harmonized IFAD's evaluation function with those of other IFIs. One change was for IOE to discontinue the resource-intensive project evaluations and introduce project completion report validations (PCRVs) and project performance evaluations (PPEs) on a selective basis.

Following the peer review, IOE also expanded its Evaluation Manual, originally issued in 2009, to include dedicated indicators for assessing the performance of IFAD-funded projects on gender, climate change and scaling up of projects.

These indicators were presented to the Evaluation Committee in November 2010 as part of the progress report on the implementation of the peer review's recommendations. These and other changes to IFAD's evaluation system were incorporated in the 2011 revised Evaluation Policy.

The Evaluation Cooperation Group*

The ECG was established in 1996 to harmonize evaluation standards by developing and disseminating common approaches to evaluation, following an assessment of the five major multilateral development banks: the African Development Bank, the Asian Development Bank, the European Bank for Reconstruction and Development, the Inter-American Development Bank and the World Bank.

The ECG has adopted a framework for assessing evaluation independence along four dimensions: (i) behavioural autonomy, which refers to the ability and willingness to report candidly, uncompromisingly and transparently; (ii) organizational independence, i.e. the independent evaluation unit must report directly to an oversight body and not to management, and have control over its human resources, work programme and budget; (iii) protection from outside interference in the design and implementation of an evaluation, and (iv) avoidance of conflict of interest, i.e. the evaluators must be free from previous involvement with programmes, activities or entities being evaluated.

The ECG report, *Serving a Changing World: Report of the Task Force on Multilateral Development Banks (1996)*, stated that a 'determined effort should be made to harmonize performance indicators and evaluation criteria, taking into account the differing circumstances of each institution'. It further called on the heads of the multilateral development banks' evaluation units to meet on a regular basis to exchange experience, with this purpose in mind.

IOE qualified for membership on the basis of its independence from IFAD Management and the size, diverse membership and status of IFAD as both an IFI and a specialized United Nations agency. ECG members and observers meet twice a year (spring and autumn) to discuss and share experiences on current evaluation issues. The meetings are hosted by the ECG Chair, the role of which rotates among ECG members. For 2017, IFAD is the chair of the ECG.

Promoting evaluation harmonization. To promote evaluation harmonization among multilateral development banks, the ECG has developed and uses Good Practice Standards and benchmarking studies to assess the extent to which these standards are applied by its members. They cover the following areas: Country Strategy and Programme Evaluation; Policy-Based Lending Operations Evaluation; Private Sector Operations

Evaluation; Public Sector Operations Evaluation; Review Framework for the Evaluation Function (Peer Reviews); and Technical Assistance/Cooperation Evaluation.

While there are some differences among the members of the ECG, most have adopted similar approaches to evaluations of public and private sector projects, as well as sectoral, thematic and country-level evaluations. The ECG has expanded its role to serve as a forum for these organizations to share ideas and experiences, coordinate their work and publish joint projects.

* www.ecgnet.org.

The relevance of IOE's work, and the importance of its independence from IFAD Management, has been recognized in such peer reviews as the 2010 ECG report and, more recently, the 2013 survey and document review by the Multilateral Organisation Performance Assessment Network, a network of like-minded donor countries.

IFAD's Revised Evaluation Policy (2011)

In May 2011, the IFAD Evaluation Policy[4] was revised and approved by the Executive Board to provide further clarification and guidance on the purpose and role of independent evaluation at IFAD. While the fundamental principles – independence, accountability, partnership and learning – and operational policies of the 2003 Evaluation Policy remain largely valid, the new Policy incorporates the recent changes that have taken place in IFAD since this first Evaluation Policy, such as the approval of the Fund's direct supervision and implementation support policy, and the introduction of country presence. The revision also reflects the most up-to-date evolution of the evaluation function in development organizations, in particular within other international financial institutions.

A distinct new feature of the 2011 Evaluation Policy is the integration of IFAD's self-evaluation system. The Policy for the first time stipulates the definition and policy provisions of IFAD's self-evaluation functions. The revision also refers to the new Terms of Reference and Rules of Procedure of the Evaluation Committee approved in May 2011,[5] which, inter alia, redefine the objectives and scope of work of the Committee as well as its oversight responsibilities in relation to IFAD's evaluation function.

Subsequent amendments to the Evaluation Policy were approved by the Executive Board in December 2013, April 2014, and September and December 2015 on issues such as revision of the procedures for selecting and appointing the director, revision of the procedures for handling disciplinary measures following integrity investigations, and the revised timeline for the ARRI of IFAD Operations.

Reflections on the Journey of the Office of Evaluation from a Studies-Oriented Unit to a Fully-Fledged Independent Outfit

By Mona Bishay, former IFAD staff member until 2008: Senior Economist, Senior Evaluator, Deputy Director of the Office of Evaluation and Studies in 2004, and Director of the Near East, North Africa and Europe Division

Getting the Most out of Independence

I first worked in IFAD's evaluation division when it was still reporting to IFAD Management, and then again after it became independent. When independence was established in 2003, its impact on the Office of Evaluation and Studies was significant: evaluators were empowered. Evaluators still had to think twice about what they wrote, and act with great institutional consideration and care, but they were able to delve more deeply into what was happening on the ground. This is really the cornerstone of accountability, and there is no learning without accountability: an institution cannot learn unless evaluation can tell it like it is.

From the advent of evaluation independence until the time I left the Fund in 2008 – at which time I was Director of the Near East, North Africa and Europe Division – I witnessed mounting credibility of the evaluation function and evaluators gaining more appreciation in the institution, in particular with the country programme managers. This was achieved because the institution's confidence in the evaluators' impartiality and professionalism had been greatly enhanced. Evaluators and their operational partners succeeded in opening up rather than working in silos.

How to gain credibility and respect? As a starting point in any evaluation, evaluators need to emphasize what has worked on the ground. They should start from the positive achievements and successes of a project/programme/strategy/policy, and give credit where credit is due, that is to IFAD's operations staff and their country partners who worked together to achieve the success. Moreover, evaluators need to thoroughly understand the country and local socio-economic context and appreciate the constraints faced by operations on the ground. This comes, among other things, from fully interacting with partners and stakeholders and giving enough time to the evaluation missions in the field. Poverty reduction is the art of the possible; nothing is carved in stone. Therefore, evaluators need to maintain flexible perspectives in order to fully appreciate the difficulties embedded in specific contexts.

Another essential element is for evaluations to propose few, doable and realistic recommendations based on a system of prioritization of what is more important for the poor, for the country, and for IFAD.

How Rigour and Structure Have Improved the Evaluation Function

During its first years IFAD evaluators did not have to follow a unified methodology. Internationally agreed evaluation criteria (relevance, efficiency, effectiveness, etc.) were not used in a systematic manner, and it was difficult, if not impossible, to aggregate findings across evaluations. In fact, there was no across-the-board attempt to assess performance using criteria that reflected IFAD's specificity. Very soon, it was realized that criteria reflecting the specific nature of IFAD have to be systematically assessed to develop a realistic view of the effectiveness of IFAD as a development organization. Today, these criteria are part and parcel of what IFAD has become.

Following the independence of IFAD's evaluation function, the Independent Office of Evaluation developed a rigorous evaluation methodology that was conceived and developed to be very IFAD-specific. This is reflected in the mandatory requirement to assess the impact of IFAD's interventions on rural poverty and to focus on gender, empowerment, innovation and scaling up (in addition to the conventional evaluation criteria). This was a big leap forward for IFAD as it allowed the institution to have a solid evaluation methodology that is tailored to its unique mandate.

Another important innovation was the implementation of an evaluation rating system. Although there are problems associated with ratings, their implementation allowed the evaluation function to have more credibility and rigour, and in particular to aggregate results and make them comparable over time and for various types of interventions (see Figure 2.1).

B. Key Structural Features

The independent evaluation function, with the support of IFAD Management, has increased the credibility of evaluations at IFAD and is seen by governing bodies and the public at large as an assurance that the institution is accountable and that it is working to improve itself and its results. It is also increasingly seen as an effective tool to continuously strengthen the Fund's mandate and to improve, through its recommendations, the design of projects and country strategies and programmes.

IOE and the Executive Board and Evaluation Committee

A key feature of IFAD's independent evaluation function is the working relationship which IOE has with the Executive Board and the Evaluation Committee, which together form the authorizing environment for IOE to function efficiently and effectively. Their roles include reviewing IOE's annual

Figure 2.1. Key milestones and evaluations in the evolution of IOE.

work programme, recommending approval of its budget to the Governing Council, and making other recommendations to fine-tune IOE's performance.

The Executive Board oversees IFAD's evaluation work and assesses the overall quality and impact of IFAD's operations as documented in evaluation reports. The Board members are drawn from Member States and elected for a three-year term. Their meetings are presided over by IFAD's President.

The Board is assisted by the Evaluation Committee. The Evaluation Committee was established in 1987 as a permanent subsidiary body of the Executive Board, which performs in-depth reviews of selected evaluation issues and IOE's strategies and methodologies. It discusses selected evaluation reports and also makes suggestions to the Committee to include evaluations of particular interest in IOE's annual work programme.

The Committee is composed of nine members chosen from the 36 members on the Executive Board. Committee members are elected for a three-year term and drawn from OECD countries, and the Organization of Petroleum Exporting Countries and list of developing countries.

For years, the Evaluation Committee undertook annual country visits to locations where IOE had conducted CPEs, in order to gain first-hand knowledge and experience of the work of IFAD in the country and to provide more informed guidance on strategic, operational and evaluation matters. Since 2014, these visits have been organized by IFAD's Secretariat and undertaken by selected Executive Board members, to enable a broader involvement of Member States' representatives in the work of IFAD.

IFAD's Evaluation Committee: Focusing on What Works, What Does Not Work, and How IFAD Can Better Serve People Living in Rural Poverty

By Margot Skarpeteig, former Deputy Permanent Representative of the Kingdom of Norway to IFAD from September 2014 to May 2017. During this period, Ms Skarpeteig represented the Kingdom of Norway in the Evaluation Committee.

I have been a member of IFAD's Evaluation Committee for three years, on behalf of Norway. The nine members are elected by IFAD's Executive Board for a three-year term of office. We meet four times a year and review the findings and recommendations of completed evaluation reports, discuss how IFAD's evaluation office can further strengthen its work, and suggest new evaluations and evaluation methodologies.

My membership in the Evaluation Committee has been the highlight of my work as Deputy Permanent Representative of Norway of the UN Agencies in Rome. There are several reasons for this.

First, the small size of the committee makes it possible for all perspectives to be shared and deliberated. IFAD Management, IFAD's Independent Office of Evaluation and the committee members bring their perspectives forward. The discussions are always refreshing – open, interactive and frank.

Second, the governance structure ensures independence of IOE, since it reports to the Executive Board instead of to IFAD Management. The Evaluation Committee is a sub-committee of the Board, and we are tasked to perform in-depth reviews of selected evaluation issues and look into strategies and methodologies of the evaluation office and provide our views to the Executive Board. We have helped the Executive Board and IFAD Management to make timely and appropriate decisions and have ensured that evaluation findings are integrated into IFAD's programmes and policies.

Last but not least, at our meetings we always discuss substance. We focus on what works, what does not work, and how IFAD can better serve people living in rural poverty. With the same goal in mind, we focus on how IOE can further strengthen its methodologies and enhance the quality of its reports, in line with requirements of the UN Evaluation Group. I like to think of the Evaluation Committee as IFAD's change agent, always trying to make IFAD deliver better towards eradicating rural poverty and food insecurity.

C. Evolving Methodology

In the early years at IFAD, evaluators did not follow a unified methodology for project evaluation. Internationally agreed-upon evaluation criteria (such as relevance, efficiency and effectiveness) were employed, but not in a systematic manner. It was difficult, if not impossible, to aggregate findings across evaluations. There was no rigorous, universal attempt to assess performance using criteria such as impact, sustainability, gender, innovation and performance of IFAD and partners, which today are recognized as key elements in social and economic development. Eventually, evaluators realized that they could not ignore such dimensions to develop a realistic view of the development effectiveness of the organization as a whole.

Following the independence of IFAD's evaluation function, the office developed an evaluation policy and a rigorous evaluation methodology.

The manual was first issued in 2009, in keeping with the principles spelled out in the Evaluation Policy. The Evaluation Manual aims to ensure consistency, rigour and transparency in independent evaluations.

A second edition was released in 2015, seeking to renew, update and consolidate current guidelines in order to achieve even higher-quality standards in IFAD evaluations. The revision of the manual was undertaken in recognition of the dynamic environment in which IFAD operates and in response to the evolution in the approaches and methodologies used in international development evaluation. The second edition expands the section on evaluation fundamentals to include the concepts of theory of change (TOC) and more explicit impact pathways, and reflects the core methodologies for evaluations which were not contemplated in the first edition, including corporate-level evaluations (CLEs), impact evaluations and evaluation synthesis reports. Aligned with the Sustainable Development Agenda, the second edition also introduces evaluation criteria and indicators on natural resources management and adaptation to climate change to be applied in the evaluation of all IFAD-financed operations.

This more refined approach, combined with the conventional evaluation criteria, led to a major leap forward for IFAD, as it allowed the institution to have a solid evaluation methodology that was perfectly tailored to its unique mandate. In addition, IOE and the Programme Management Department (PMD) of IFAD signed methodological harmonization agreements allowing both to use the same criteria and sub-criteria, thus facilitating the comparison between self-evaluations and independent evaluations.

Table 2.1 below summarizes the main modifications from the first edition to the next, whereas Appendix 1 discusses in detail methodological fundamentals.

Evaluation Criteria

IOE uses evaluation criteria which build on the Organisation for Economic Co-operation and Development/Development Assistance Committee (OECD/DAC) Glossary of Key Terms in Evaluation and Results-Based Management;[6] the United Nations Evaluation Group's (UNEG) Norms and Standards;[7] and the ECG's Good Practice Standards for the Evaluation of Public Sector Operations.[8] Taken together, these criteria allow for a solid assessment of the key aspects of IFAD initiatives to be made, and also enable comparison with peers who apply similar criteria to judge performance and therefore enables benchmarking. IOE has introduced additional evaluation criteria[9] which allow it to assess key dimensions that are specific to IFAD's work and operating model.

IOE uses a number of core questions for each evaluation criterion to help conduct performance assessments and ensure consistency in the foundation for ratings. These core questions have been carefully crafted, based on the internationally recognized definition of each evaluation criterion.

The evaluation criteria used by IOE and their definitions are shown in Table 2.2 below. However, it should be kept in mind that not all criteria are necessarily relevant to all types of evaluations. Appendix 2 discusses the evaluation criteria used by IOE, key questions and ratings.

Evaluation Ratings

For each criterion, IFAD evaluations apply scores on a six-point scale, according to the practices of most evaluation offices of international financing banks. This is a symmetric system of ratings, i.e. there are three positive (from 4 to 6) and three negative (from 1 to 3) scores: 1 = very unsatisfactory; 2 = unsatisfactory; 3 = moderately unsatisfactory; 4 = moderately satisfactory; 5 = satisfactory; 6 = very satisfactory. There is no neutral score (simultaneously not negative and not positive), and evaluators must come to conclusions based on clear arguments.

In the discussions on evaluation methodology, two main arguments against the use of ratings often appear: first, that scores are subjective assessments; and

Table 2.1 Main modifications between the first and second editions of the Evaluation Manual.

Features	*First edition of the Evaluation Manual (2009)*	*Second edition of the Evaluation Manual*
Evaluation products	• Project evaluations (completion evaluations and interim evaluations) • Country programme evaluations (CPEs) • Corporate-level evaluations • Annual Report on Results and Impact of IFAD Operations (ARRI)	• Project completion report validations • Project performance evaluations • Impact evaluations • Country strategy and programme evaluations (CSPEs) • Corporate-level evaluations • Annual Report on Results and Impact of IFAD Operations (ARRI)
Chapters	I Background II Methodological fundamentals III The project evaluations methodology IV The country programme evaluation methodology	I Background II Methodological fundamentals III Evaluation criteria, key questions and ratings IV Project completion report validation V Project performance evaluation VI Country strategy and programme evaluation VII Corporate-level evaluation VIII Impact evaluation IX Evaluation synthesis report X Communication, dissemination and learning
Evaluation criteria	**Project evaluations and portfolio performance in CPEs** • Project performance (relevance, effectiveness and efficiency) • Rural poverty impact (household income and assets, human and social capital and empowerment, food security and agricultural productivity, natural resources and the environment, institutions and policies) • Other performance criteria (sustainability, and promotion of pro-poor innovation, replication and scaling up)	**Project evaluations and portfolio performance in CSPEs** • Rural poverty impact (household income and assets, human and social capital and empowerment, food security and agricultural productivity, and institutions and policies) • Project performance (relevance, effectiveness, efficiency, and sustainability of benefits) • Other performance criteria (gender equality and women's empowerment, innovation and scaling up, environment and natural resources management, and adaptation to climate change)

Table 2.1 (continued)

Features	*First edition of the Evaluation Manual (2009)*	*Second edition of the Evaluation Manual*
	• Overall project achievement (relevance, effectiveness, efficiency, rural poverty impact, sustainability, innovation, replication and scaling up) • Partner performance (IFAD, government, cooperating institution, non-governmental organization/ community-based organization)	• Overall project achievement (rural poverty impact, relevance, effectiveness, efficiency, sustainability of benefits, gender equality and women's empowerment,* innovation and scaling up,** environment and natural resources management, and adaptation to climate change) • Partner performance (IFAD and government)
	Country programme evaluations • Non-lending activities (policy dialogue, partnership building and knowledge management) including grants • Performance of the country strategic opportunities programme (COSOP) (relevance, effectiveness) • Government and IFAD partnership (portfolio performance, non-lending activities, and COSOP performance)	**Country strategy and programme evaluations** • Non-lending activities – policy dialogue – partnership-building – knowledge management – South–South and Triangular Cooperation and reimbursable technical assistance • COSOP performance (relevance, effectiveness) • Government and IFAD partnership (portfolio performance, non-lending activities, and COSOP performance)
Rating	Six-point scale	Six-point scale

* Climate change and gender quality and women's empowerment were included following the 2010 peer review of IOE by the ECG.

** In 2017, IOE and IFAD Management signed a Harmonization Agreement of IFAD's Independent Evaluation and Self-Evaluation Methods and Systems. As a result, 'innovation and scaling up' will be rated as two separate criteria in future evaluations.

Source: Evaluation Manual 2015b.

second, that they run the risk of provoking excessive discussions about the numbers, thus detracting from the substantive issues. While these arguments are partially valid, there are two reasons that justify the use of ratings in IFAD's evaluations:

(i) The adoption of a standard methodology and common questions, as well as the 'peer review' processes of evaluations, contribute to generating coherent guidelines among evaluators and to limiting subjectivity. Likewise, the ratings offer a clearer synthesis to readers and users of the evaluations, especially when the analysis includes positive and negative observations. In such cases, the scores allow the 'tie' to be broken and allow for a more transparent evaluation.

(ii) With regard to potential disputes over scores, they do not necessarily divert from the discussion of substantive issues if the evaluators use such debates to better explain or strengthen their arguments. IFAD Management adopted the rating system as a tool to strengthen its internal self-evaluation system and measure its results.

A Mix of Methods

IOE generally prefers to apply a mix of evaluation methods – combining the breadth of quantitative methods with the depth of qualitative approaches. A mixed-method approach tends to yield greater validity than using any one method, and is also in line with UNEG good practices.

Alternative Methodological Approaches

In the literature on evaluation, there are alternative approaches to making comparisons between a sample project and a control sample. These approaches are valuable because in most evaluations it is not possible to conduct new large surveys. In addition, in some cases institutional changes being evaluated are unique phenomena for which control groups cannot be established.

Some alternative methods are based essentially on a review of the 'logical framework' or 'TOC' of the interventions evaluated. These are reinforced with an empirical investigation of the basic hypotheses of the projects and of the intervention processes and mechanisms. Examples of these are:

(i) the 'realistic' approach (Pawson and Tilley 1997), which seeks to identify the 'working mechanisms' of interventions and how they interact in different contexts to produce different effects on the various actors;

(ii) the 'causal contribution analysis' (Mayne 1999, 2001, 2008), which is based on a TOC and operates by determining whether the project's performance conforms to the logical stages of that theory and whether the intermediate results are compatible with those foreseen (see section on contribution analysis); and

(iii) the 'general elimination method' (Scriven 2008), in which the evaluator formulates alternative hypotheses to explain the observed effects and progressively eliminates those which are less plausible, thus taking into account the context in which the intervention has been performed.

Most IFAD evaluations attempt to use these approaches to examine the logical coherence and identify the key assumptions of project design, and to determine

Table 2.2 Definition and rating of the evaluation criteria used by IOE.

Criteria	*Definition*	*Mandatory*	*To be rated*
Rural poverty impact	Impact is defined as the changes that have occurred or are expected to occur in the lives of the rural poor (whether positive or negative, direct or indirect, intended or unintended) as a result of development interventions.	X	Yes
	Four impact domains		
	• Household income and net assets: household income provides a means of assessing the flow of economic benefits accruing to an individual or group, whereas assets relate to a stock of accumulated items of economic value. The analysis must include an assessment of trends in equality over time.		No
	• Human and social capital and empowerment: human and social capital and empowerment include an assessment of the changes that have occurred in the empowerment of individuals, the quality of grass-roots organizations and institutions, the poor's individual and collective capacity, and in particular, the extent to which specific groups such as youth are included or excluded from the development process.		No
	• Food security and agricultural productivity: changes in food security relate to availability, stability, affordability and access to food and stability of access, whereas changes in agricultural productivity are measured in terms of yields; nutrition relates to the nutritional value of food and child malnutrition.		No
	• Institutions and policies: the criterion relating to institutions and policies is designed to assess changes in the quality and performance of institutions, policies and the regulatory framework that influence the lives of the poor.		No

(*Continued*)

Table 2.2 (continued)

Criteria	*Definition*	*Mandatory*	*To be rated*
Project performance	Project performance is an average of the ratings for relevance, effectiveness, efficiency and sustainability of benefits.	X	Yes
Relevance	The extent to which the objectives of a development intervention are consistent with beneficiaries' requirements, country needs, institutional priorities and partner and donor policies. It also entails an assessment of project design and coherence in achieving its objectives. An assessment should also be made of whether objectives and design address inequality, for example, by assessing the relevance of targeting strategies adopted.	X	Yes
Effectiveness	The extent to which the development intervention's objectives were achieved, or are expected to be achieved, taking into account their relative importance.	X	Yes
Efficiency	A measure of how economically resources/ inputs (funds, expertise, time, etc.) are converted into results.	X	Yes
Sustainability of benefits	The likely continuation of net benefits from a development intervention beyond the phase of external funding support. It also includes an assessment of the likelihood that actual and anticipated results will be resilient to risks beyond the project's life.	X	Yes
Other performance criteria			
Gender equality and women's empowerment	The extent to which IFAD interventions have contributed to better gender equality and women's empowerment, for example, in terms of women's access to and ownership of assets, resources and services; participation in decision making; work load balance and impact on women's incomes, nutrition and livelihoods.	X	Yes
Innovation	The extent to which IFAD development interventions have introduced innovative approaches to rural poverty reduction.	X	Yes

Table 2.2 (continued)

Criteria	*Definition*	*Mandatory*	*To be rated*
Scaling up	The extent to which IFAD development interventions have been (or are likely to be) scaled up by government authorities, donor organizations, the private sector and others agencies.	X	Yes
Environment and natural resources management	The extent to which IFAD development interventions contribute to resilient livelihoods and ecosystems. The focus is on the use and management of the natural environment, including natural resources defined as raw materials used for socio-economic and cultural purposes, and ecosystems and biodiversity – with the goods and services they provide.	X	Yes
Adaptation to climate change	The contribution of the project to reducing the negative impacts of climate change through dedicated adaptation or risk reduction measures.	X	Yes
Overall project achievement	This provides an overarching assessment of the intervention, drawing upon the analysis and ratings for rural poverty impact, relevance, effectiveness, efficiency, sustainability of benefits, gender equality and women's empowerment, innovation, scaling up, as well as environment and natural resources management, and adaptation to climate change.	X	Yes
Performance of partners			
• IFAD	This criterion assesses the contribution of partners to project design, execution, monitoring and reporting, supervision and implementation support, and evalu ation. The performance of each partner will be assessed on an individual basis with a view to the partner's expected role and responsibility in the project life cycle.	X	Yes
• Government		X	Yes

Source: Evaluation Manual 2015b.

whether the necessary conditions have been met to generate expected results and impacts.

Particularly for the theory-based evaluations, understanding the TOC[10] is critical. The TOC may be explicitly stated or, as is often the case, is implicit and therefore needs to be articulated and clarified. A TOC articulates how activities are linked to outcome and impact, clearly outlining the assumptions behind, including the implicit assumptions. Assumptions would pertain to external influence, for example, or the assumed behavioural effect of a particular intervention on the target group. It should also capture assumptions about the distributional effects of the interventions in terms of anticipated project benefits to different groups, based on gender, age, geographical location, etc.

The purpose of a TOC is to describe how an intervention leads to results. A TOC illustrates, generally both in graphic and narrative form, the series of assumptions and links underpinning the presumed causal relationships from input to impact; it describes the pathways to change. A TOC also has to factor in the context, something that is often missing in classical logframes but is essential for understanding when, how, why, and under what conditions certain actions lead to certain outcomes, or not, i.e. it is to a very large degree tailored for learning purposes. In this respect, a distinction can be made between programme-level and project-level change. The former would apply, for example, to initiatives aiming at reforms that might facilitate entry into higher value-added areas of production, enhance systemic climate resilience, etc., while the latter might aim, for example, at delivering a set of inputs designed for a beneficiary group of farmers who were not previously using that input. In the former, evaluation tools would need to be able to capture systemic and institutional change, whereas in the latter, the evaluation tools would need to identify uptake, whether beneficiaries understand and trust the technology/input, and whether they have sufficient skill and knowledge.

Theory of Change

In evaluation, the gathering of evidence and formulation of questions are intrinsically linked to an understanding of how specific interventions lead to results and, thus, how those results can be measured for insight into the effectiveness of programmes, policies and strategies.

IFAD's unique role in contributing to inclusive and sustainable rural transformation is built on what is known as a theory of change or TOC. The TOC was explicitly articulated in the context of the Tenth Replenishment of IFAD's Resources (IFAD10) and included in IFAD's Results Measurement Framework (RMF), and is broken down into the following five levels:

1. **Global poverty, food security and agricultural investment outcomes** – embodies the broader development goals to which IFAD contributes, tracked by measures of extreme poverty, food insecurity and investment in agriculture.
2. **Country-level development outcomes and impact** – assumes that success in achieving global poverty and food security targets is predicated on development projects, such as those supported by IFAD, and is measured by the number of people moving out of poverty.

3 **Country-level development outputs delivered by IFAD-supported projects** – underpins the achievement of impacts and outcomes reflected by the number of people lifted out of poverty. The supply of project outputs enables smallholders to overcome key constraints, giving them access to a range of productive resources and inputs (e.g. knowledge, infrastructure, markets, financial and business services, and responsive institutions). The number of people using the services provided by IFAD-supported projects is considered the most important indicator at this level.
4 **Operational effectiveness of IFAD-supported country programmes and projects** – assesses the performance of IFAD-managed processes aimed at positively influencing the design, delivery and achievement of programme outputs. The assumption is that enhancing the quality and efficiency of IFAD's business model and associated processes will lead to improved programme outputs. Achievement of agreed programme results is supported by: better project design responding to the needs and priorities of poor rural people; an effective portfolio management process identifying underperformance in time for a course of correction; proactive assistance to relevant entities for project implementation; and deepening knowledge of how policies for smallholder agriculture and rural development work in practice.
5 **IFAD's institutional effectiveness and efficiency** – reflects a commitment to ensuring institutional effectiveness and efficiency in the ways the Organization mobilizes, allocates and utilizes its financial and human resources. The assumption is that strong performance in this area will focus resources on what adds most development value, with overall impact and quality delivered for less, in terms of expenditures.

A TOC may be developed based on past evaluations or theoretical and empirical research on processes of change in similar interventions. It may also be derived from the intervention's existing logical framework; however, it must be developed not merely based on a document describing the logframe, but based on critically seeking out, and articulating, plausible explanations for the anticipated changes that can be tested through the evaluation questions and for which evidence may be found. This said, it should also be kept in mind that use of TOC is a fairly recent phenomenon in IFAD. Therefore, an explicit TOC may not be available in many policies, strategies or operations, and reconstructing the TOC is not always an easy task. In newer projects, it is to be expected that an explicit TOC has been developed, as the TOC is not only an evaluation tool, but is also recognized as an excellent tool for stakeholder dialogue in project preparation. Strong input from stakeholders and beneficiaries is required, and therefore the process leading to the articulation of the TOC is important.

A robust dialogue with stakeholders will help build ownership, clarify the assumptions, confirm the plausibility of the TOC, and give visibility to those assumptions that are implicit; it can shed light on the possible discrepancy between what is written in various documents and what is the reality. This process is time-consuming, may be costly, and is not applicable in all cases. Sound judgement should therefore be exercised in determining the necessity and scope of the exercise. In some cases, it is advisable to keep the TOC simple, to use the logframe and make the tacit hypotheses clearer and highlight gaps. However, it should also be noted that as experience is gained, and with systematic sharing of experience and building up a knowledge base, it will be less time-consuming and the quality of the TOC in IFAD documents may improve.

Contribution Analysis

The 'contribution analysis' approach suggested by John Mayne[1] is an approach that has been used in a number of IFAD evaluations. According to Mayne, there are six iterative steps in contribution analysis, each step building the contribution story and addressing weaknesses identified in the previous stage:[1]

Step 1: Set out the attribution problem to be addressed. Too often the question of attribution is ignored in programme evaluations. Observed results are reported with no discussion as to whether they were the result of the programme's activities. At the outset, it should be acknowledged that there are legitimate questions about the extent to which the programme has brought about the results observed.

Step 2: Develop the TOC and the risks to it. The key tools of contribution analysis are TOC and results chains. With these tools the contribution story can be built.

Step 3: Gather existing evidence on the TOC. Assess the logic of the links in the TOC. Reviewing the strengths and weaknesses of the logic, the plausibility of the various assumptions in the theory, and the extent to which they are contested will give a good indication of where concrete evidence is most needed. Gather the evidence. Evidence to validate the TOC is needed in three areas: observed results, assumptions about the TOC, and other influencing factors.

Step 4: Assemble and assess the contribution story and the challenges to it. The contribution story, as developed so far, can now be assembled and assessed critically. Questions to ask at this stage are: Which links in the results chain are strong (good evidence available, strong logic, low risk and/or wide acceptance) and which are weak (little evidence available, weak logic, high risk and/or little agreement among stakeholders)? How credible is the story overall? Does the pattern of results and links validate the results chain? Do stakeholders agree with the story – given the available evidence, do they agree that the programme has made an important contribution (or not) to the observed results? Where are the main weaknesses in the story? For example: Is it clear what results have been achieved? Are key assumptions validated? Are the impacts of other influencing factors clearly understood? Do any weaknesses point to where additional data or information would be useful?

Step 5: Seek out additional evidence and identify what new data are needed. Based on the assessment of the robustness of the contribution story in Step 4, the information needed to address challenges to its credibility can now be identified – for example, evidence regarding observed results, the strengths of certain assumptions, and/or the roles of other influencing factors. It may be useful at this point to review and update the TOC, or to examine more closely certain elements of the theory.

Step 6: Revise and strengthen the contribution story. New evidence will build a more credible contribution story, buttressing the weaker parts of the earlier version or suggesting modifications to the TOC. It is unlikely that the revised story will be foolproof, but it will be stronger and more credible. Contribution analysis works best as an iterative process. Thus, at this point the analysis may return to Step 4 and reassess the strengths and weaknesses of the contribution story. Statements of contribution at this level attempt to provide factual evidence for at least the key parts of the entire TOC.

1 By exploring the contribution the programme is making to the observed results, one can address the attribution of the programme to the desired results. Mayne focuses on clearly defining the TOC, modelling it, and revisiting it regularly across the life of the programme.

Harmonization Agreement between IFAD's Independent Evaluation and Self-Evaluation

One of the keys to enhancing the effectiveness and usefulness of evaluations is to harmonize methods and systems used in independent evaluation with those used in self-evaluation. The harmonization agreement between IFAD's independent evaluation and self-evaluation methods and systems has been in place since 2006.

Without the harmonization of their methodologies, no comparative analysis could be undertaken on the findings and ratings of the self-evaluation and independent evaluation systems. This would, in turn, hinder the verification of self-evaluation information.

Revisions. In December 2016, the Fund's Executive Board paved the way for the second revision of the agreement in ten years. At the Board's request, and in keeping with the Evaluation Policy (2011), IOE and IFAD Management (represented by PMD and the Strategy and Knowledge Department [SKD]) prepared the revised harmonization agreement.[11]

The update was especially timely, given the publication of the second edition of the IFAD Evaluation Manual (2015b), the adoption of the Development

Effectiveness Framework,[12] and the issuance by management of new operational procedures on project logical frameworks, completion reporting and country strategies.

Standards. In order to ensure that the two systems are mutually reinforcing, the agreement explicitly builds on the Good Practice Standards of the ECG, internationally agreed-upon principles for managing for development results, as well as on the principles of the original harmonization agreement and guidance provided by IFAD Governing Bodies. Moreover, the experience of other IFIs was reviewed in order to learn from past experience and good practices in other organizations whose realities are applicable to the IFAD context.

Evaluation criteria. The OECD/DAC evaluation criteria are the basis of the self-evaluation and independent evaluation systems at IFAD. As such, the core evaluation criteria in the second edition of the IFAD Evaluation Manual and the Operational Procedures on Completion Reporting (2015b) build on the OECD/DAC Glossary of Key Terms in Evaluation and Results-Based Management, which are typically adopted by both the self- and independent evaluation functions of other IFIs. The manual also includes other evaluation criteria (e.g. gender equality, innovation and scaling up) which are specific to IFAD's mandate and respond to the increased attention paid by governments to results monitoring.

Rating scale. Both the self-evaluation and independent evaluations will continue to use the same six-point scale rating system. Self- and independent evaluations will no longer provide individual ratings for the four impact sub-domains in the areas of priority for rural transformation promoted by IFAD, namely: (i) household incomes and assets; (ii) human and social capital and empowerment; (iii) food security and agricultural productivity; and (iv) institutions and policies. Self- and independent evaluations will continue to rate overall rural poverty impact to enable comparisons and tracking of trends over time.

Harmonization at the project level. Independent PCRVs, PPEs, and impact evaluations and self-evaluation reports at the project level (i.e. project completion reports [PCRs]) will follow the same set of criteria and definitions.

PCRs, PCRVs, PPEs and impact evaluations will assess *ex post* the validity of the assumptions made at design. PCRs, PPEs and impact evaluations will examine in greater detail the TOC of the project, describing the intended pathways to change and the actual ones as demonstrated through the project implementation experience.

A complementary function exists between the independent impact evaluations conducted by IOE and the impact assessments conducted by IFAD Management (SKD). Impact evaluations by IOE are performed only on completed IFAD-financed operations and from an entirely independent perspective. They cover all the evaluation criteria included in the Evaluation Manual, including the rural poverty impact criterion. Impact assessments conducted by IFAD Management primarily focus on the impact criterion and include *ex ante* impact assessments using experimental and non-experimental methods, which requires impact assessment methods and processes to be embedded in programme design and the close involvement of management in data collection and analysis throughout implementation. PCRs will continue to report on impact for all operations, although there may be differences in the assessment techniques between projects that are subject to impact assessment and those that are not.

Harmonization at the country level. Independent evaluations at the country programme level (i.e. country strategy and programme evaluations [CSPEs]) will follow the criteria and definitions set forth in the 2015 second edition of the Evaluation Manual. While CSPEs will continue to assess portfolio performance according to project evaluation criteria, they will give special emphasis to the assessment of the relevance and effectiveness of the country strategic opportunities programme (COSOP) and of non-lending activities (e.g. country-level policy engagement, knowledge management and partnership-building).

However, self-evaluations at the country programme level (i.e. COSOP completion reviews) will focus on the assessment of relevance and effectiveness of the COSOP (as opposed to the project level) and provide a rating for the same. This assessment will summarize key findings from the performance of the portfolio (without a detailed analysis of all the project-level criteria), including non-lending activities. When a COSOP Completion Review is available, the concerned regional division will not be required to prepare a new self-assessment as part of the CPE. Scope for further harmonization of methodologies at the country level may exist.

Adaptive management. Independent evaluations will adopt the project logical framework and the COSOP results framework (objectives, indicators and targets) defined at approval stage as the reference for their assessment. If the frameworks or targets have been modified, independent evaluations will take the latest change as the main reference, provided that the changes in logframes and results frameworks are adequately justified and documented in accordance with established relevant procedures. The approach papers and evaluation reports will indicate which project logical framework and COSOP results framework will be subject to evaluation.

The Harmonization Agreement between Independent and Self-Evaluation in IFAD

By Ashwani K. Muthoo, Director, Global Engagement, Knowledge and Strategy Division of IFAD and former IOE Deputy Director (2011–2016)

More than a decade ago, IFAD recognized the need to harmonize its self- and independent evaluation systems as an instrument for promoting accountability and learning. For this purpose, IFAD first introduced a harmonization agreement between PMD and IOE in 2006. The initial agreement was further enhanced and revised in 2011 and 2017.

The broad purpose of the harmonization agreements is to ensure that the two systems generate credible and comparable information on the performance of IFAD operations in all regions. The agreements have also helped clarify the mutually reinforcing roles of IFAD Management and IOE, which, together with the Evaluation Committee and Executive Board, are responsible for ensuring that IFAD has a robust and comprehensive evaluation architecture.

The harmonization agreements have ensured that the self- and independent evaluation methodologies are aligned – for example, in terms of assessment criteria, rating scales and timing of reports. This has contributed to improving the general quality of self- and independent evaluations and improved the usefulness of all evaluations undertaken by IFAD, whether by management or IOE.

The first two harmonization agreements were between PMD and IOE. However, over time it was realized that a more broad-based agreement was required with IFAD Management, especially given the increasing role played by other departments (e.g. SKD) in furthering IFAD's results, knowledge and development effectiveness agenda. Therefore, the 2017 harmonization agreement reflects a more comprehensive institutional agreement between IFAD Management and IOE.

The introduction of the harmonization agreements also presented some challenges – for instance, in making sure that concerned staff are properly trained in specific methodologies and processes to enable the timely and effective implementation of the agreements. Sensitizing Executive Board members (especially the Evaluation Committee) has also been important, in order for them to be properly equipped to provide strategic guidance and oversight of IFAD's wider evaluation function.

The focus of the first harmonization agreement of 2006 was on the assessment criteria, rating scales and timing of reports. The objectives of the 2006 harmonization process were to:

(i) Ensure that the self-evaluation and independent evaluation systems generate comparable information for reporting to IFAD Management and the Executive Board;
(ii) Streamline existing self-evaluation systems to generate a comparable set of data that is consistent, while at the same time realizing efficiency gains; and
(iii) Enable IOE to increasingly focus on higher-plane evaluations (i.e. beyond the project level), once the self-evaluation system is considered reliable at the project level.

The need to enhance the 2006 harmonization agreement was motivated by the introduction of the revised IFAD Evaluation Policy in May 2011, which called for IOE to introduce new products such as PCRVs and PPEs.

Building on the 2006 agreement, the 2011 harmonization agreement included additional provisions for:

(i) **Results-based country strategic opportunities programmes:** Management will follow the same methodology for COSOP completion reviews as contained in the Evaluation Manual for CPEs. This includes using and rating the same three key criteria – portfolio performance; non-lending activities (i.e. knowledge management, policy dialogue and partnership-building); and COSOP performance (in terms of relevance and effectiveness); and

(ii) **The President's Report on the Implementation Status of Evaluation Recommendations and Management Actions (PRISMA):** Although there is no ACP for PCRVs and PPEs, starting from its 2011 edition the PRISMA includes a new section reporting on the follow-up to the recommendations that Management found feasible in the PCRVs and project performance assessments (now called PPEs). The PRISMA will also include an inventory, in matrix format, of recommendations not adopted by Management and a brief explanation as to why they were not found pertinent.

The introduction of the second edition of the IOE Evaluation Manual (2015b) and the Development Effectiveness Framework (2016) by IFAD Management brought about the need for a new harmonization agreement. The new agreement was developed between the end of 2016 and beginning of 2017. One distinguishing feature of this agreement was that it took a fresh look at IFAD's evaluation methods and processes in both the self- and independent evaluation systems. It also benefited from a comprehensive assessment of the experiences and lessons of similar agreements in other international financial institutions.

Among other issues, in developing the 2017 harmonization agreement, a common understanding was generated on the definition of all evaluation criteria applied by IFAD Management and IOE, including the underlying questions in assessing operational performance by criteria. The agreement also committed the organization to reassess the number and nature of evaluation criteria to be used in the future, as a means to streamline and improve the efficiency of IFAD's overall evaluation architecture.

In conclusion, having a harmonization agreement between self- and independent evaluation has clearly demonstrated that evaluation is a shared responsibility, and therefore it is important that both parties are equally on board. Having a solid and well-designed harmonization agreement should help to further strengthen IFAD's self-evaluation activities. This could also lead to recalibrating the use of IOE resources towards higher-plane evaluations, to generate lessons on systemic and thematic issues for better development effectiveness.

D. IOE Evaluation Products

The range of IOE evaluation products ensures that the fundamental dimensions of evaluation – accountability and learning – are adequately covered. IOE's evaluations look at IFAD's performance and impact at the corporate, country and project levels (International Fund for Agricultural Development, 1999, 2002, 2003a, 2003b, 2004, 2013, 2015a, 2015b, 2015c, 2016a, 2016b).

First Evaluation Products

In the early years, evaluation products at IFAD focused on **mid-term evaluations** (since the first projects had yet to be completed). The mid-term evaluations were typically undertaken at around the mid-life of project implementation and generally related to the 50 per cent disbursement mark. Once time had passed and projects were nearing completion, **completion evaluations** were introduced. They were conducted after the finalization of the PCR that was prepared by the borrower or by the cooperating institution (when IFAD operated with the support of 'cooperating institutions'). These evaluations were generally conducted six to 18 months after a project's closing date.

Interim evaluations were also introduced as a required step before embarking on a second phase of a project, or before launching a similar project in the same region. The findings, recommendations and lessons learned from these evaluations served as the basis for the design of subsequent interventions. Three to five years after a project had closed, ***ex post* evaluations** were conducted to assess the sustainability of the project's interventions.

Thematic studies and evaluations were also introduced to examine IFAD's experience related to a specific aspect or theme that cross-cut a country or region. **Focused evaluations** were also used to concentrate exclusively on one component or aspect of a project/programme or group of projects in a country. Instead of this type of studies or evaluations, IOE may now undertake thematic CLEs.

Innovating through Evaluation Work

By Paolo Silveri, Lead Regional Economist and Country Programme Manager at IFAD's Latin America and the Caribbean Division and former IOE Senior Evaluation Officer (1994–2005)

The main role of the evaluation function at IFAD has always been to ensure an external, qualified and analytical look at the Fund's operations, to express an independent opinion on what had happened during implementation and why, and to recommend ways to overcome, in future projects and programmes, the main issues identified by the evaluation teams. While engaging in such a strategic function, the Office of Evaluation in its various configurations (Office of Evaluation and Studies, Office of Evaluation, Independent Office of Evaluation) has often identified and disseminated innovating tools and success stories that contributed significantly to the Fund's reputation as an agent of rural transformation and a promoter of innovative approaches to local development in marginal and vulnerable areas.

In 1999, the Assistant Vice President of PMD asked IOE to support the Fund in developing an effective tool to foster M&E in IFAD-supported projects, in light of the generally unsatisfactory performance of the projects' M&E function despite repeated efforts and budget allocations to improve the Fund's effectiveness in this area. Between 1999 and 2000, IFAD's global experience in M&E was analysed and the outcome of the stock-taking was presented to the Executive Board in April 2000. In the following two years, multidisciplinary and multilingual technical teams worked in all regions of IFAD operations to create IFAD's first Practical Guide for Project M&E, a modular manual to support the Fund's project management units worldwide in establishing and managing M&E systems more effectively. The Guide, published in 2002, was adopted as an IFAD basic document, translated into all IFAD official languages and distributed at loan negotiations for several years. Unofficial translations were also carried out in Brazil, China, Iran and Viet Nam. While M&E still represented a challenge for many IFAD-supported projects, considerable progress was made in explaining in simple terms the basic elements of M&E and in consolidating the state-of-the-art practical knowledge on project M&E into a single, user-friendly publication. Fifteen years after its creation, it is still being used in several parts of the world, and a proposal to produce an updated version of the Guide is being discussed at IFAD, upon the initiative of the Fund's Policy and Technical Advisory Division.

In 2000, the (then) Office of Evaluation and Studies launched a thematic evaluation on Organic Agriculture in Latin America and the Caribbean (LAC). The evaluation included both IFAD- and non-IFAD-supported experiences to promote certified organic agriculture in six countries throughout LAC, identifying the potentials and challenges of a largely unknown market. While barely considered in IFAD's menu at project design, organic agriculture presented clear and untapped comparative advantages for most of the Fund's target group, by being 'organic by default', as well as having considerable growth potential – the organic market was worth over US$10 billion per year at the time, and was growing at double-digit rates.

The thematic evaluation highlighted the pros and cons of entering organic agriculture markets, shedding light on the networks, the various niches (e.g. fair trade, Green Agriculture, uncertified organic, local certifications) and offering insights on how to overcome some of the major market barriers at entrance. The evaluation was published in 2003 and was followed by similar ones on India and China in 2005. The evaluations' results were presented at a global seminar at IFAD, followed by invitations to present them in Washington (World Bank, IFAD North American liaison office and Capitol Hill), Eschborn (Deutsche Gesellschaft für Internationale Zusammenarbeit), Rome (international conference at the Municipality [Campidoglio]), New Delhi (co-hosted by the Ministry of Agriculture of India and the National Cooperative Development Corporation), Beijing (co-hosted by the Ministry of Finance of China) and several capitals in LAC. Today, organic agriculture is mainstreamed into IFAD's core business, and many projects worldwide support its development, mainly with youth and in partnership with the private sector.

In 2004, another ground-breaking thematic evaluation was carried out on Innovative Experiences in IFAD Projects in Peru. The evaluation identified repeated patterns and methodologies throughout various projects already evaluated in Peru, explaining the reasons for their success. The evaluation results were also published in a book (De Zutter, 2004) and disseminated through libraries and bookshops, giving IFAD-initiated rural transformation methodologies in the Andes an unprecedented diffusion in the area. Today, IFAD's experiences and methodologies are well known for having been replicated and scaled up through their integration in public policies and the government's investment programmes throughout the Highlands of Peru.

These are only a few examples that show how, historically, evaluation work at IFAD has gone well beyond its essential function of independent evaluation, and how it has contributed to strengthening and disseminating two of IFAD's distinctive assets – innovation and knowledge-sharing – for which the Fund is appreciated by its members worldwide, which recognize that effective innovations and methodologies, through policy dialogue, replication and scaling up, multiply IFAD's effectiveness and contribution to sustainable development goals (SDGs) beyond what its limited resources allow it to achieve as a result of its direct investment.

Currently, IOE's evaluation products include PCRVs, PPEs, impact evaluations, CSPEs, CLEs, evaluation synthesis reports and the ARRI of IFAD Operations.

Project Evaluations

Since 2011, IOE's approach to project evaluations has consisted of undertaking **PCRVs and project performance assessments** (now called **PPEs)**, in lieu of interim and completion evaluations, which were extremely costly and time-consuming. Undertaken after an IFAD-funded operation has been completed, both evaluations assess results and impact to promote accountability and learning, but only PPEs generate recommendations that can inform other projects that IFAD funds.

Project Completion Report Validations

A PCRV is a desk-based validation of a PCR, which contains an assessment of the results and impact of an IFAD-financed project or programme, including ratings for each evaluation criterion covered in the validation. PCRs are prepared by recipient governments, following guidelines developed by IFAD Management, within six months after the project completion date.

A PCRV involves an extensive documentary review, including that of the relevant COSOP, all the relevant project documents and monitoring reports, and key policy and strategy documents to assess the relevance criteria. The validation usually begins by clarifying and articulating the conceptual framework for the project, if one was not already specified in the design. In this context, there is a review of the final project design to understand its overall project objectives, the type of components the project seeks to support, its underlying assumptions, cost structure and institutional arrangements, and the overall project strategy.

Sample PCRV Checklist

Scope

- To what extent have all the chapters, including relevant annexes foreseen in the PCR Guidelines, been adequately covered?

Data

- To what extent is the PCR based on robust data?
- Are the data collected adequate for their intended use and has their reliability been ascertained?
- If M&E and Results and Impact Management System data were limited, were supplementary surveys and research carried out?
- Are data systematically analysed to provide information needs in a valid manner?

Lessons

- To what extent have lessons been drawn from a) project design and b) project implementation?
- Are lessons based on explicit evaluation findings?

Process

- To what extent has the PCR process been inclusive of all relevant stakeholders?

Candour

- To what extent is the narrative objective?
- To what extent have both positive and negative results been reported?
- To what extent is the rating coherent with the narrative?

PCRVs include findings on performance and ratings across the evaluation criteria adopted by IOE. They contribute to strengthening a key component of a project's self-evaluation system, namely, the PCR. The PCRV also includes an overall assessment of the quality of a PCR. They feed into and inform the design of new projects, in addition to the implementation of ongoing projects, and thus contribute to enhancing the quality of IFAD operations in general. PCRVs, however, do not include recommendations and, as such, do not require IFAD Management's response.

Project Performance Evaluations

The objectives of a PPE are to assess the results of the project under consideration; generate findings and recommendations for the design and implementation of ongoing and future operations in the country involved; and identify issues of corporate, operational or strategic interest that merit further evaluative work.

The two basic building blocks for PPEs are the PCRV and a field visit, which includes discussions with multiple stakeholders (e.g. government officials, project staff, beneficiaries, co-financiers) and visits to selected project sites. The PPE takes into account factors such as the presence of novel aspects in a project and the quality of the data. A PPE may be preferred, for example, when the validation has found a lack of important data or a discrepancy between evaluation of the closure report and that of the independent validation; and when there is the need to provide sources of information for future evaluations.

While missions provide PPEs with additional evidence and information, they also face challenges. In particular, country visits are often conducted under time and budgetary constraints, and as a consequence it may be difficult to collect new primary data related to impact. Therefore it is important to recall the purpose of the PPEs and note that they are expected, primarily, to fill important information gaps. They are not expected to investigate all activities financed under projects/programmes or to undertake in-depth impact assessments.

PPEs contribute to enhancing the quality of IFAD's operations in general, and constitute an important building block for the preparation of key IOE evaluation products, such as the ARRI, evaluation synthesis reports, and other evaluations such as CSPEs and CLEs.

Impact Evaluations

A new kind of evaluation made its debut at IFAD in 2013, when IOE introduced **impact evaluations**, in keeping with a decision of the Executive Board. Impact evaluations are intended to assess the performance and impact of an IFAD project in a more quantitative and rigorous manner, and provide recommendations for future operations. Impact evaluations allow IOE to learn and gain hands-on experience in addressing the challenges of complex, multi-component, rural development programmes and projects. Conducting an impact evaluation underscores how critical this type of evaluation can be to strengthening IFAD's organizational accountability and learning, better informing decision-making, and improving performance of future operations (Felloni and Somma, 2015).

Impact evaluations are conducted once every year, resources allowing, and are now considered one of IOE's key products. (See also 'Synthesis and consolidation of findings' later in this publication.)

It is important to note that IOE conducts *ex post* impact evaluations, either at the time of project completion or some years later. Being involved in interim and/or *ex ante* impact evaluations would compromise the independence of IFAD's evaluation function.

IOE's First Impact Evaluation

By Fabrizio Felloni, IOE Deputy Director

The impact evaluation of the Dry Zone Livelihood Support and Partnership Programme in Sri Lanka (2013) was the first conducted by IOE and one of the first project assessments at IFAD involving extensive primary data collection. It consisted of a qualitative survey (41 focus group discussions with beneficiaries and 30 interviews with key informants from project staff and local governments) as well as quantitative data collection, covering over 2,560 households (with and without project).

Among the challenges faced in undertaking this evaluation were:

- Data availability gaps: (i) the loss of electronic data from an earlier baseline survey; (ii) reliability of monitoring data due to project staff turnover and limited data quality assurance;
- Methodological issues: (i) difficulty in identifying a proper comparison group due to likely spill-over effects from target groups to non-target ones (e.g. the adoption of new crop varieties or of new livestock rearing practices); (ii) the time required to observe results (most interventions had begun two years or less before the evaluation).

The survey shed light on targeting: it showed that the project had focused on villages with less access to basic infrastructure and, within these villages, on households with a lower asset base, although with slightly better educational status and more diversified cropping patterns. In order to address selection bias, the evaluation used: (i) propensity score matching (to compare project and comparison households sharing similar observed characteristics); and (ii) the Heckman correction model.

Compared with the project's own M&E data, independent analysis shows more mixed socio-economic impacts. Households assisted by the project financed investments in dairy farming and higher-value crops out of their own savings and had to forego the purchase of other household assets or reduce other categories of expenses.

This first impact assessment led to broader methodological observations. First, since IFAD projects are targeted at specific geographic areas, communities (and sometimes specific household groups within these communities), it is challenging to find comparison sites and households that share salient characteristics with those supported by projects. Second, IFAD projects are multi-component and these components are not implemented in the same way in all the sites. Thus the logical chain of cause and effect is fuzzy to model and assess. Third, econometric results are not always self-explanatory; they need to be interpreted and can yield inconsistent results, and this is why combining quantitative and qualitative techniques makes an important hermeneutical contribution.

Country Strategy and Programme Evaluations

Background. IOE undertook its first country portfolio evaluation in 1992, which focused on assessing the results of IFAD-funded projects and programmes, and following a decision of the Executive Board. These were not intended to evaluate each project but to provide comparative information on the most essential aspects of project performance, and to develop strategic and operational orientation for IFAD's future project pipeline in the country. In mid-1999, CPEs were introduced, replacing country portfolio evaluations, which led to a number of improvements, especially in the development of new COSOPs, which remain the major vehicle for IFAD's engagement at the country level. CPEs were given the broader remit of assessing the results of both IFAD-funded projects and programmes and, though in less detail, non-lending activities.

With the introduction of the second edition of the Evaluation Manual, CPEs were renamed **country strategy and programme evaluations**, starting with the CSPEs undertaken by IOE in 2016. CSPEs cover the full range of IFAD support to a country, including lending and non-lending activities, including grants, South–South and Triangular Cooperation and reimbursable technical assistance as well as country programme and COSOP management processes. Specific attention is devoted to assessing strategic dimensions of the IFAD–government partnership in promoting rural transformation.

Each year IOE conducts several evaluations at the country-programme level, covering each geographical region of IFAD. These assessments cover the operations and strategic lines of IFAD and its partners in the countries concerned,[13] generally during the previous decade. They are carried out before IFAD and the government concerned formulate a new collaborative strategy or COSOP, benefiting from the findings and recommendations of the evaluation.[14]

CSPEs assess government and IFAD cooperation under three main levels of analysis: (i) reviewing project portfolio performance, applying the evaluation criteria for each project; (ii) assessing 'non-lending' activities (i.e. knowledge management, partnership-building and policy engagement); and (iii) assessing IFAD's strategic performance (relevance and effectiveness of the COSOP).

CSPEs assess the relevance of the COSOP in terms of geographic and socio-economic targeting, consistency with country strategies and IFAD's strategic institutional framework, objectives, and alignment between objectives and the resources available to achieve them. In addition to strategic relevance, programme evaluations examine strategic effectiveness, that is, the extent to which the specific objectives of the COSOP have been achieved through projects and other activities carried out by the government, IFAD and its partners.

Evaluation of the loan portfolio requires work similar to project-level evaluations (cabinet study, field visits and further validation with key informants). The review of non-lending activities requires a 'mapping' exercise of: (i) IFAD's intervention sub-sectors and public policies that are most relevant to IFAD-funded programme; and (ii) the main actors in these sub-sectors (national and international institutions, civil society organizations, private entrepreneurs, research institutions). This makes it possible to identify ongoing collaborations, as well as the opportunities not yet exploited in terms of knowledge management, development of relationships with partners and dialogue on public policies. For example, in a country programme evaluation in Rwanda, the evaluation team met with those responsible for American and British cooperation, respectively, on the issues of support for coffee production cooperatives and reforms in the micro finance/rural finance sub-sector. While there was enormous potential for knowledge-sharing and joint work between IFAD and other donors in the dialogue on relevant sectoral policies, the evaluation identified untapped opportunities, which it addressed in its findings and recommendations.

In another example, in a country programme evaluation in Ecuador, the mission in the country provided an opportunity to verify the important progress of the newly created Rural Dialogue Group, made up of eminent political and academic figures from Ecuador. The evaluation noted how this group, supported by an IFAD grant, had been devised to foster dialogue between civil society and the government and acknowledged its great potential to influence the governmental policy agenda regarding rural development.

In addressing the strategic performance assessment, most evaluations at the country level find limited data regarding the follow-up of the strategic objectives outlined in the COSOP. Often, therefore, evaluation teams need to develop a logical 'map' by establishing links between lending and non-lending activities on

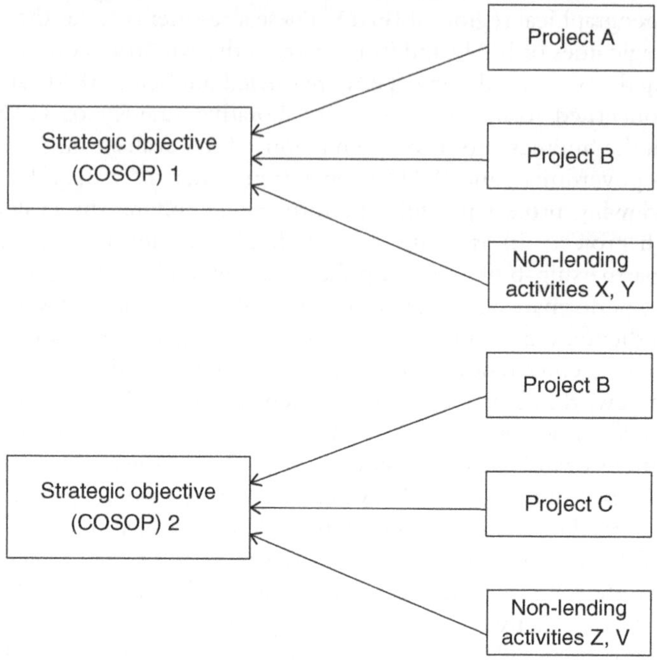

Figure 2.2. Theoretical map of the correspondence between COSOP objectives and lending and non-lending activities.

Source: Felloni, *et al.*

the one hand, and the objectives of the COSOP on the other. This makes it possible to infer progress on the individual objectives of the COSOP (see Figure 2.2).

Country Programme Evaluations

By Khalid El Harizi, former Senior Evaluation Officer at the Office of Evaluation and Studies (March 1991 to October 1999), where he was in charge of the first four CPEs ever carried out by IFAD

The appointment of the late Dr Pierre Spitz as head of the Office of Evaluation and Studies in 1990 resulted in a major change in the orientation of the office's work, which shifted its focus from M&E systems to evaluation and thematic studies. This shift clearly reflected the research background of Dr Spitz but also stemmed from the evolving needs of IFAD.

During the 1990s, evaluations generally brought an independent perspective to project performance that represented quite a shock to an institution that did not yet have an evaluation culture. While evaluations addressed accountability concerns, they adopted a strategic perspective, emphasizing learning and, in particular, understanding how projects interacted with their environments. In fact, IFAD was the first international organization to conduct country evaluations. The World Bank's first country evaluation was performed in 1995 and it mainstreamed them in 1998, whereas other organizations started country evaluations in the 21st century.

The Gulf War of 1991 had an unexpected and long-lasting impact on the evaluation function. The Executive Board of IFAD, faced with a new project to approve for Yemen (which had just reunited), requested a country-wide evaluation of the numerous projects previously approved for Yemen. Subsequently, it was decided that all countries with seven or more projects should undergo a CPE. Three countries immediately qualified: Bangladesh, Sudan and Yemen.

These initial CPEs were faced with a daunting task of building the information base necessary to conduct the evaluations, as there was a dearth of project evaluations available, few effective M&E systems and none of the communication and digital technologies that are available today. They required evaluation teams with strong analytical capabilities and substantial time and budgets to carry out the necessary information-gathering, which involved retrieving information from archives and visiting all projects in a country in order to assess them on the ground.

The main impact of CPEs has been to strategically shape IFAD operations in a given country, with this impact lasting sometimes over a decade. Yemen and Sudan CPEs (1992–1993) demonstrated that IFAD had missed its main target (the rural poor) by following the lead of the World Bank and focusing on irrigated areas. In Mauritania (1997–1998) the CPE used a new approach to rural poverty analysis, which emphasized social exclusion. This was in sharp contrast with the prevailing analysis, which emphasized income per capita. The new approach enabled IFAD to break a taboo regarding the descendants of slaves, whom the report designated by their particular type of settlement (Adwabas). IFAD and the government followed up with a project targeting this large group of people.

All early CPEs directly inspired the formulation of new country strategic opportunities papers (as the COSOPs were then called), which led to what is now a standard practice and requirement of linking the formulation of new COSOPs to the outcome of CPEs. CPEs also pioneered the organization of high-profile national stakeholder conferences to widely discuss their outcomes and gain ownership of CPE's conclusions and recommendations at country level.

CPEs, together with other types of project evaluations (Mid-Term and Completion evaluations in particular), created a corporate culture of evaluation and improved the targeting of IFAD operations. CPEs assessed both lending and non-lending operations, so they provided an opportunity to learn lessons that took into account IFAD's overall contribution in a country (some CPEs showed that non-lending operations, particularly grants, played an important role in the struggle against rural poverty at the country level). They also reduced IFAD's dependency on the analytical capabilities of cooperating institutions. In fact, at a time when IFAD depended on cooperating institutions for project supervision, evaluations represented the main source of institutional learning.

However, at times the impact of evaluations was limited by resistance to change inside and outside IFAD. At country level, the absence of a window of opportunity to implement evaluation recommendations could also be a limiting factor. Windows of opportunity open when the evaluation coincides with a political need to redefine rural and agricultural development strategies. These favourable situations are generally the exception rather than the rule.

Gains in evaluation culture and knowledge can actually be reversed or lost. If not used in the few months after an evaluation is completed, the evaluation results retain an academic or historical interest but lose a large part of their operational worth. The rate at which institutional memory is lost increases with time and staff turnover. In addition, the shift towards development effectiveness and the emphasis on accountability that characterized the 2000s, combined with a budget crunch, have contributed to a loss of corporate analytical capability as far as the evaluation function is concerned.

In sum, the capacity of CPEs to facilitate institutional learning and change should be considered at three levels. At the level of borrowing governments, it is the demand for CPEs at the specific moment they are carried out that determines their usefulness and impact. At IFAD corporate level, it is through their credibility and ability to foster a culture of evaluation that CPEs have had their major impact. Finally, for both IFAD and governments, CPEs have been instrumental in shaping their cooperative programme and gearing the proceedings of the loans more deliberately towards the rural poor and the excluded.

Corporate-Level Evaluations

IOE introduced CLEs in the 1990s to assess the results of IFAD-wide corporate policies, strategies, business processes or related organizational aspects. They generate findings and recommendations that can be used to formulate more effective corporate policies and strategies, or to improve business processes and organizational architecture.

Evaluation Syntheses

Evaluation syntheses were introduced by IOE in 2012, after the 2010 ECG peer review of IFAD's Office of Evaluation and Evaluation Function. The peer review had recommended this new product as a way to further strengthen the use of evaluation findings, learning and feedback loops.

Evaluation syntheses take stock of findings from previous independent IOE evaluations, bringing together lessons learned and capturing evaluation-based lessons from other organizations. They are knowledge products that aim to enhance the general understanding of a particular topic and strengthen IFAD's evaluation feedback and learning loops; this level of abstraction makes them more useful in highlighting the strategic implications of findings and raising strategic issues for further consideration by IFAD Management and the governing bodies. Synthesizing existing evaluation evidence allows evaluation synthesis reports to contribute to decision-making processes in an effective way, especially when there is neither adequate time nor resources to undertake a fully-fledged evaluation.

Annual Report on Results and Impact of IFAD Operations

The ARRI, presented for the first time to the Evaluation Committee and the Executive Board in September 2003, consolidates the evaluations of IFAD operations that IOE has completed, and has become IOE's annual flagship report. Aiming to provide an integrated perspective across all types of evaluations, the report provides highlights of trends, issues, lessons and challenges that are important for the Fund to recognize and understand in order to enhance its operational effectiveness. The ARRI contains the aggregate performance assessment of all evaluations conducted in a given year and normally covers all five IFAD geographic regions. Each edition also includes a dedicated section on one learning theme.

Fifteen Years of the ARRI

To date, IOE has published 15 issues of the ARRI. Its longevity is a reflection of IFAD's continued commitment to strengthening accountability and transparency in reporting on results, as well as learning for better impact on the ground. By identifying systemic and cross-cutting issues to improve IFAD's development effectiveness, the ARRI is a fundamental instrument of IFAD's overall evaluation architecture. Over the years, the ARRI has contributed to strengthening IFAD's results culture.

The 15 years of preparing the ARRI have also made IOE's evidence base more robust. The 2017 ARRI draws its findings from a sample of 295 project evaluations which were completed between 2002 and 2016 as well 40 CSPEs, using a common methodology. The collection of 1953 ratings from IOE project evaluations allows IOE to perform new analyses. As a result, the 2017 ARRI confirms a statistically significant improvement in IFAD's project performance between the Eighth and the Ninth Replenishment of IFAD's Resources.

In addition, the ARRI concentrates on the learning issues which are recurrently emerging in IOE's evaluations as areas that merit further attention. For instance, the first learning theme was introduced in 2007 and focused on innovation and sustainability. Other learning themes have highlighted issues related to project-level M&E, natural resources management, efficiency, direct supervision, policy dialogue, project management and, in 2016, knowledge management. In 2017, the learning theme focuses on financial management and fiduciary responsibilities in IFAD-supported operations.

When the ARRI was first produced in 2003, IFAD was one of the very first development organizations to produce a report of this type. In fact, the Fund remains one of the very few multilateral and bilateral organizations to produce an annual evaluation similar to the ARRI.*

* The Independent Evaluation Department of the Asian Development Bank and the Independent Evaluation Group of the World Bank also produce annual reports similar to the ARRI.

Communication Tools and Dissemination

Disclosure of evaluation results is a core principle of IFAD's Evaluation Policy, which states: 'IOE shall ensure that all evaluation reports and other evaluation products are disclosed to the public and disseminated widely using electronic and other media.' And it goes on to stress that accountability through evaluation analysis requires that successes, unexpected results, shortcomings and failures highlighted during the evaluation be disclosed to relevant partners and the general public without interference from any vested interest, thus stressing the independence aspect of IOE's work.

On the more traditional dissemination agenda, two key factors deserve attention when discussing dissemination. One is the emergence of new information technology-based and virtual platforms for sharing lessons from all types of evaluations and evaluation products; the other is the recognition of the need to more systematically share findings with the intended beneficiaries of IFAD assistance and with media and civil society in developing countries. In this respect, the integration in IOE of a dedicated Evaluation Communication Unit (ECU) is a considerable strength. The ECU undertakes communication functions, with a view to enhancing IOE's profile as a knowledge producer and to reach out and share evaluation learning. The Unit implements a standard dissemination approach for each type of product. A targeted dissemination strategy may also be developed for specific evaluations, or for specific audiences, especially the beneficiaries.

The most commonly used communications tools are: publications and other material (Profiles, Insights, overviews, reports, newsletters); Internet (website, social media); media relations (press releases); audiovisual tools that are particularly suited to reaching the main beneficiaries; and events (in-house and international). The ECU collaborates with IFAD's Communications Division and is continually exploring the use of innovative communications techniques, strategies and instruments to improve IOE communications and learning tools.

Below is a short description of the communication tools that IOE produces:

Audiovisuals

- **Infographics.** IOE develops visually engaging infographics to allow readers to easily understand the most important findings and recommendations of an evaluation.
- **Videos**. IOE may produce videos that accompany evaluation reports to show the highlights of an evaluation and illustrate beneficiary perspectives in relation to the evaluation results and activities on the ground.

Publications

- **Evaluation Insights** focus on one learning issue emerging from evaluations, with the aim of generating further debate about the selected issue among development practitioners.
- **Evaluation Profiles** are two-page summaries of the main conclusions and recommendations from an IOE evaluation. Evaluation Profiles are prepared for CLEs and CSPEs, evaluation synthesis reports and impact evaluations.
- **Evaluation reports** are shared electronically with internal and external audiences, including IFAD Management and staff, IOE staff and consultants, members of the Executive Board, UNEG, ECG, the concerned IFAD regional network (e.g. IFADAsia, FIDAFRIQUE, KARIANET), evaluation associations and other networks according to the geographical region. The lead evaluator disseminates the evaluation report to government officials and other in-country partners. If there is an IFAD country office, it supports IOE in disseminating hard copies of evaluation reports, including to subnational authorities and related partners in remote areas. On an exceptional basis, and resources permitting, a learning event may also be organized at the country level.
- **Newsletter.** IOE publishes a quarterly newsletter (at the end of March, June, September and December), which also includes updates related to the Evaluation Committee and the Executive Board.
- **Overview booklets**. This short-format publication is intended for those who do not have time to read the evaluation report in its entirety. It comprises an overview or summary and IFAD Management's response or the ACP, depending on the type of evaluation.

Internet

- **Website.** In cooperation with the Communications Division and within the framework of IFAD's corporate website, IOE maintains a dedicated website (www.ifad.org/ evaluation) that is used as the main channel to publish evaluation reports and publications, announce events and post news, newsletters and editorials. It is also used to disseminate updated versions of documents such as the Evaluation Policy and the Evaluation Manual.

- **Social media** has changed how people communicate, and organizations now also use these channels as advocacy tools to inform the public about their work. IOE uses social media to disseminate reports that are published on the IOE website and announce events. It does so by using IFAD's social media accounts (e.g. Twitter, Facebook, IFAD social reporting blog) and its own Twitter account.

Media Relations

Press releases: the Evaluation Policy states that

> on a case-by-case basis, IOE will issue a press release to inform the wider audience of the main results and lessons from key evaluations. IOE will be responsible for preparing the press release and will not require clearance from anyone outside the division for the contents contained therein.

Press releases are normally used to announce the launching of selected evaluation reports (in particular CLEs and CSPEs) but may be used in other cases, for instance to communicate important events that may be of interest to the media.

Events

Emerging evaluation findings are presented at in-house learning events for ARRIs, CLEs, evaluation synthesis reports and impact evaluations. For CSPEs, as a final step in the evaluation process, national workshops for the evaluation stakeholders are held in partner countries to discuss main issues emerging from CSPEs. The workshops are co-organized by IOE and the concerned ministry in the country, in cooperation with PMD. The ECU develops and implements a communication strategy for these workshops, which includes a media advisory note and a press release.

The purpose of these in-house and country-level events is to stimulate discussion around the evaluation and its main findings and recommendations. Also, they present an opportunity for IOE to display and share various publications.

Notes

1 Rapid External Assessment 1994, www.ifad.org/documents/10180/6321d376-8a1a-4536-ae08-e5867fa0f043.
2 From 1999 to 2011, IOE project evaluations included an ACP.
3 www.ifad.org/documents/10180/d3021cee-9b78-41d7-82ad-a44f98760de8.
4 www.ifad.org/pub/policy/oe.pdf.
5 www.ifad.org/documents/10180/8bf5dc2e-ad32-4564-96d3-8d6661613829.
6 www.oecd.org/development/evaluation/2754804.pdf.
7 www.uneval.org/document/detail/22.

8 www.ecgnet.org/document/good-practice-standards-evaluation-public-sector-operations.
9 Innovation and scaling up (which are now rated separately following the 2017 harmonization agreement between IFAD's independent evaluation and self-evaluation), gender equality and women's empowerment, environment and natural resources management and climate change.
10 Mayne (2015).
11 www.webapps.ifad.org/members/ec/96/docs/EC-2017-96-W-P-4.pdf.
12 www.webapps.ifad.org/members/eb/119/docs/EB-2016-119-R-12.pdf.
13 While other partners such as international organizations, and non-governmental and civil society organizations intervene as well, the overall cooperation agreement is established between IFAD and the government.
14 As per the Executive Board's decision, if a CSPE has been undertaken by IOE, its ACP must be included as an annex to the COSOP submitted for consideration by the Board. This allows the Board to assess whether the CSPE findings and recommendations have been adequately included in the COSOP. In addition, when a COSOP is presented to the Executive Board and a CSPE has been conducted prior to that COSOP, IOE will also present the CSPE to the Executive Board.

References

Attiga, A.A., Head, I.L., Piñeiro, M.E., Rovani, Y. and Sene, D. 1994. Rapid External Assessment of the International Fund for Agricultural Development. The Challenge of Rural Poverty: The Role of IFAD. Rome: IFAD.

De Zutter, P. 2004. Diez Claves de Éxito para el Desarrollo Rural. Lima: MARENASS, CORREDOR, FIDA and PREVAL.

Evaluation Cooperation Group. 2010. Peer Review of IFAD's Office of Evaluation and Evaluation Function. Rome: ECG.

Felloni, F. and Somma, S. 2015. Impact Evaluations in Rural Development: Opportunities and Challenges. The Emerging Experience of IFAD's Independent Office of Evaluation. Evaluation Matters, Second Quarter. African Development Bank. 82–93.

International Fund for Agricultural Development. 1999. New Evaluation Process. IFAD website: www.ifad.org/evaluation/policy_and_methodology/tags/2085736. Rome: IFAD.

International Fund for Agricultural Development. 2002. A Guide for Project M&E. Independent Office of Evaluation of IFAD. Rome: IFAD.

International Fund for Agricultural Development. 2003a. Evaluation Policy. Independent Office of Evaluation of IFAD. Rome: IFAD.

International Fund for Agricultural Development. 2003b. The Adoption of Organic Agriculture among Small Farmers in Latin America and the Caribbean. Thematic Evaluation. Independent Office of Evaluation of IFAD. Rome: IFAD.

International Fund for Agricultural Development. 2004. Experiencias innovadoras en los proyectos del FIDA en la República del Perú. Thematic Evaluation. Independent Office of Evaluation of IFAD. Rome: IFAD.

International Fund for Agricultural Development. 2013. IFAD's Independent Evaluation: Ten Years of Accountability, Learning and Transformation. Independent Office of Evaluation of IFAD. Rome: IFAD.

International Fund for Agricultural Development. 2015a. Annual Report on Results and Impact of IFAD Operations. Independent Office of Evaluation of IFAD. Rome: IFAD.

International Fund for Agricultural Development. 2015b. Evaluation Manual. Independent Office of Evaluation of IFAD. Rome: IFAD.

International Fund for Agricultural Development. 2015c. The Evolution of the Independent Evaluation Function at IFAD. Independent Office of Evaluation of IFAD. Rome: IFAD.

International Fund for Agricultural Development. 2016a. Annual Report on Results and Impact of IFAD Operations. Independent Office of Evaluation of IFAD. Rome: IFAD.

International Fund for Agricultural Development. 2016b. Overview. Independent Office of Evaluation of IFAD. Rome: IFAD.

Mayne, J. 1999. Addressing Attribution through Contribution Analysis: Using Performance Measures Sensibly. Ottowa : Mimeo, Office of the Auditor General of Canada.

Mayne, J. 2001. Addressing Attribution through Contribution Analysis: Using Performance Measures Sensibly. *Canadian Journal of Program Evaluation* 16(1), 1–24. Gatineau: CJPE.

Mayne, J. 2008. Contribution Analysis: An Approach to Exploring Cause and Effect. ILAC Brief 6. Institutional Learning and Change Initiative. Rome: ILAC.

Mayne, J. 2015. Useful Theory of Change Models. *Canadian Journal of Program Evaluation* 30(2), 1–12. Gatineau: CJPE.

Pawson, R. and Tilley, N. 1997. Realistic Evaluation. London: Sage.

Scriven, M. 2008. A Summative Evaluation of RCT Methodology: And An Alternative Approach to Causal Research. *Journal of Multidisciplinary Evaluation* 5(9), 11–24. Kalamazoo, MI: JMDE.

3 Influential Evaluations

A. Background

Between 1983 and 2016, IOE conducted more than 420 evaluations at the country, corporate, thematic and project levels. Over the years, some evaluations have stood out as being particularly influential, having led to far-reaching and systemic, institutional change and transformation, and thus contributing to greater development effectiveness (Felloni et al., 2014, 2016; Garcia, 2015). While IOE selects the topics of these evaluations, it ensures that each topic is also of priority to IFAD Management and the governing bodies. To be influential, evaluations must have the support of key stakeholders and address critical areas of importance to them. This increases the likelihood that the results will be put to use in improving development programmes, policies and strategies.

According to the literature, at least four types of influential evaluations can be distinguished, based on their use: **instrumental**, in which the evaluation findings are used to change the evaluand or the conditions that it is working under; **conceptual**, in which the findings are used to gain conceptual knowledge; **informative**, in which the findings are used to acquire information; and **strategic**, in which the evaluation findings are used for advocacy (Levington, 2003; Højlund, 2014).

There is ample evidence that evaluations can indeed play a central role in shaping policy and thematic priorities and improving the performance of operations and results on the ground. Examples are presented in the sections that follow.

B. External Review of the Results and Impact of IFAD Operations (2002)[1]

In 2002, an External Review of the Results and Impact of IFAD Operations (Caviezel et al., 2002) took a broad look at IFAD's impact and played an essential role in the evolution of the evaluation function. It considered, first, the results and impact achieved by IFAD-supported operations and, second, the established methodologies and processes for assessing the results and impact of IFAD-supported projects, as well as other changes introduced to enhance IFAD's focus on results.

The review confirmed that IFAD had targeted its financial and policy-dialogue interventions at the most disadvantaged populations in the world's rural areas, and that there had been some impact on poverty reduction. It further noted that IFAD had promoted innovations such as microfinance, soil and water conservation, water users' associations, self-help groups, and various forms of partnership-building.

The review also identified areas in which IFAD could make improvements – for example, by taking a more systematic approach to innovation. It also found that sustainability of benefits was lower than expected at the time of loan approval. Additionally, the External Review Team found a need to strengthen the development of analytical tools for impact assessment and to strengthen IFAD's proximity to the field.

C. United Republic of Tanzania Country Portfolio Evaluation (2002/2003)[2]

The United Republic of Tanzania Country Portfolio Evaluation played a major role in sparking the enhancement of IFAD's operating model, in particular by underscoring the need for IFAD to establish a more permanent country presence. The absence of a country presence was found to be a significant constraint in IFAD's efforts to engage more coherently in police dialogue and ensure the necessary and timely implementation support to the Fund's operations. It also was seen to hinder discussions with donors and other groups and weaken the supervision of the activities of other institutions on behalf of IFAD – for instance, in such areas as physical outputs and administration/budgeting.

D. Independent External Evaluation of IFAD (2004/2005)[3]

The Independent External Evaluation of IFAD (IEE) was the first evaluation of its kind conducted since the Fund began operations in 1978. The IEE involved the entire Organization over a period of about 18 months. Staff and Member States were able to take stock of, and reflect on, the relevance of the Fund's mission and the results and impact of IFAD's activities. It also sought to assess the effectiveness of key corporate and management processes through which IFAD's policies, programmes and projects had been developed and carried out.

The IEE was closely managed by IOE, but carried out by an external team of consultants, with advice, guidance and comments from a steering committee composed of representatives of nine IFAD Member States. During the review, Member States were kept informed throughout the evaluation period through written progress reports provided by IOE.

The main outcome of the IEE was the development by Management of an Action Plan to Enhance IFAD's Development Effectiveness, which paved the way for important structural and organizational changes, new corporate policies, and the streamlining of internal processes and procedures. It included a new framework for 2007–2010 which called for a targeting policy to more effectively channel IFAD resources where they were most needed. It also led to the establishment of new systems of quality enhancement and quality assurance with arm's-length independence and management from the Office of the Vice President.

E. Corporate-Level Evaluations

At IFAD, the most influential type of evaluations are CLEs conducted by IOE of the Fund's strategies, operations and business processes. Influential CLEs conducted since 2010 have included such themes as: innovation and scaling up; direct supervision; field presence; gender equality and women's empowerment (GEWE); efficiency of IFAD-funded operations; fragile and conflict-affected states and situations; and IFAD's decentralization experience. (See Figure 3.1.)

Evaluations on Innovation and Scaling Up

The **evaluation of IFAD's Capacity as a Promoter of Replicable Innovations (2002)**[4] was undertaken during a transitional stage for IFAD, and its far-reaching findings came as a surprise to many. The implementation of the evaluation's ACP led to some improvements in terms of creating a common understanding of innovation and its processes, ascertaining strategic commitment to innovation and synchronizing the use of IFAD's instruments (loans and grants) based on the innovation requirements. These were good steps forward although, in isolation, they did not achieve the full ambition of this evaluation. Shortly after, in 2004, the IEE, using the findings of the Innovation Evaluation, recommended that IFAD clarify its role as an innovator in policy, institutional and operational terms by being a progenitor of well-tested innovative approaches that can be replicated nationwide by others and with greater resources (IEE, 2005, page 3).

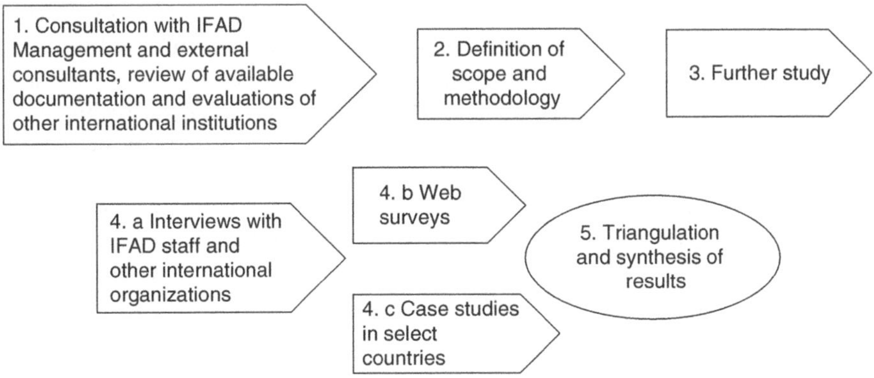

Figure 3.1 Scheme of the typical process of evaluations at institutional level.

Source: Felloni, *et al.*

In the ensuing years and in response to the IEE recommendations, IFAD implemented a new operating model with innovation and knowledge management as a main axis (IFAD's Action Plan to Increase Development Effectiveness, 2005). An IFAD strategy for innovation was developed in 2007, the grant-based instruments were upgraded to support innovation, and indicators for innovation (and scaling up) were gradually introduced in design quality assurance and implementation follow-up. These measures reflected the essence of the innovation evaluation recommendations. As such they represented a great institutional leap forward in realizing the innovation evaluation's implied vision for IFAD as a leader in promoting pro-poor replicable innovations in agriculture and rural development. This was a good reward for the evaluators!

The **evaluation of IFAD's Capacity to Promote Innovation and Scaling Up (2010)**[5] was a follow-up evaluation to assess the performance of the Fund in this area and recommend ways to improve. The evaluation found that the Fund had made concerted efforts to incorporate the promotion of pro-poor innovation into its key policy and strategy documents, and that programme performance in this domain had improved. But improvement in scaling up remained limited and some disconnect still existed between IFAD's strategic pronouncements on innovation and scaling up and its institutional capacity to deliver this on the ground. The most important evaluation recommendation was to treat scaling up as mission-critical at all stages of the programme cycle and to strengthen organizational capacities in promoting and managing the scaling up of successful innovations. Inspired by the evaluation findings and recommendations, PMD commissioned the Brookings Institution to undertake an institutional review of its scaling-up approach. This was the beginning of intensive institutional efforts to integrate scaling up more effectively in IFAD's operating model. Such efforts included: sharpening the strategic and operational emphasis on scaling up; creating a scaling-up toolkit; establishing an operational framework for scaling up; preparing thematic and country-level scaling-up notes; conducting seminars and in-house discussions on scaling up; and engaging in relevant international fora.

Not a corporate-level evaluation, but related to scaling up is the Evaluation Synthesis on **IFAD's Support to Scaling up of Results** that IOE published in 2017. The Synthesis concluded that the scaling-up journey has been long, and scaling up remains a 'work in progress'. While IFAD has emphasized scaling up at least since 2002, full conceptual clarity came only in 2015. On the positive side, the current conceptualization of scaling up is sound and draws from evaluative evidence. The Synthesis provided a set of focused recommendations for keeping up the pace of positive change, notably: (i) strengthen the country programme and project cycle to enhance scalability; and (ii) build stronger consensus and incentives in-house to support scaling up.

Direct Supervision Pilot Programme (2005)[6]

Prior to the Direct Supervision Pilot Programme, IFAD did not directly supervise the projects it funded. Instead, it delegated project supervision to selected cooperating institutions, such as the United Nations Office for Project Services. The CLE on the Direct Supervision Pilot Programme found that projects directly supervised by IFAD performed better than those supervised by cooperating institutions.

The analysis also showed that direct supervision allowed the Fund to expand its objectives of innovation, policy dialogue and partnership development. There was wide support among partners for direct supervision. As a result, IFAD moved to direct supervision of projects in what is considered to be one of the most far-reaching changes since the establishment of the Fund. The change required an amendment to the Fund's establishing agreement, which was approved by the Governing Council in 2006.

Further mention of supervision-related issues and Management's response can be found in Chapter 6 of this publication, in the discussion of the PRISMA.

Field Presence Pilot Programme (2007)[7]

This CLE assessed the performance and impact of this programme in achieving IFAD's overall objectives. While the main focus was on the three-year pilot programme in 15 countries, it also examined the experience gained with the only two out-posted country programme managers, who were located in Panama and Peru.

The objective of the pilot programme was to enhance the effectiveness of IFAD operations by focusing on four interrelated dimensions: implementation support; policy dialogue; partnership-building; and knowledge management. Prior to the pilot programme, IFAD did not have any permanent in-country presence or country office, and all activities were managed by its Rome-based staff.

The evaluation was undertaken three to four years after the launch of the pilot programme and included a comprehensive benchmarking study. The aim was to learn from the efforts and experiences of other multilateral and bilateral organizations and international non-governmental organizations that had already set up offices in recipient countries. The evaluation's conclusions and recommendations ultimately led to the establishment of an IFAD country presence programme.

IFAD's Performance with Regard to GEWE (2010)[8]

The objectives of this CLE were to: (i) assess the relevance of IFAD's strategy in promoting GEWE; (ii) learn from the experiences and good practices of other development organizations; (iii) assess the results of activities funded by IFAD related to GEWE in its country programmes and corporate processes; and (iv) generate a series of findings and recommendations that would assist IFAD's Executive Board and Management in guiding the Fund's future activities in this area. The evaluation included all departments.

The evaluation led to recommendations regarding the Organization's gender architecture itself, many of which related to reviewing and addressing staffing and corporate culture issues, including salaries, promotion, leadership positions, work-life balance and anti-harassment provisions. Other recommendations targeted planning and performance of the Fund's projects and included a call for IOE itself to enhance its capacity to assess gender issues in evaluations and country programme planning.

The CLE found room for improvement. While it called IFAD's strategic approach to gender relevant, the evaluation pointed out that guidance was fragmented among different corporate policies and other documents (e.g. strategic frameworks, the gender action plan, gender framework). These had been developed at different times and for a variety of audiences (e.g. the Executive Board, IFAD Management and staff, partners in the field).

While the objectives and main directions advocated were broadly consistent across all documents, the fragmentation made it difficult for staff at headquarters and in the field, not to mention partners in developing countries, to know which document should be considered the main reference. The evaluation also found evidence that many staff members were not fully clear on the strategic approaches advocated and how to turn these approaches into action through COSOPs and operations.

The Fund's effectiveness in meeting one of its three strategic objectives (improve women's well-being and ease their workloads by facilitating access to basic rural services and infrastructure) was found to be moderately unsatisfactory. Moreover, results of IFAD-financed operations were considered moderately unsatisfactory on the whole, even though there was significant variability across projects and countries.

A number of key corporate business processes which were essential for supporting IFAD's gender work were weak, and the evaluation found no evidence of systematic monitoring or reporting on progress related to GEWE by either Senior Management or the Executive Board, noting that reporting was largely confined to project-level activities.

In short, the overall picture of the Fund's promotion of GEWE showed a gap between rhetoric and practice. The CLE offered recommendations with a view to closing that gap. The recommendations included:

- Including a section on who within IFAD Management would be responsible for implementation, oversight and reporting.
- Producing a consolidated annual progress report, covering the results achieved in the implementation of the new policy, lessons learned and adjustments made to key corporate business processes that affect performance in gender-related activities.
- Including an overarching results measurement framework for IFAD's gender work, and specifying how the Executive Board would fulfill its role in providing guidance and support, as well as oversight on results.
- Focusing on knowledge management, learning and analytic work, and investing in building a common, evidence-based understanding among staff of the theory of GEWE and its related terminology.
- Calling for the systematic documentation and cross-fertilization of lessons learned and good practices across projects, countries and regions.

IFAD's Institutional Efficiency and Efficiency of IFAD-funded Operations (2013)[9]

In the years following the 2008 global economic and financial crisis, governments that were faced with more budget-tightening than usual cast a critical eye on efficiency in development programmes. In this context, IOE conducted a corporate-level evaluation on IFAD's efficiency (CLEE).

The CLEE covered both the efficiency of IFAD operations and the institution itself, in a number of critical areas: the management of human resources, results and budgets, information and communications technologies (ICTs), oversight and support functions, leadership and decision-making, and governing bodies.

Given its scope and coverage, it was arguably the most complex and challenging evaluation conducted by IOE. The challenge was heightened by the fact that this was the first of its kind among development agencies, requiring IOE to develop a dedicated methodology and mobilize extraordinary expertise in evaluation and a range of technical areas.

Approach. The unique features of this evaluation included the analysis of efficiency at multiple levels – output, outcome, impact and scaled-up outcome and impact. The massive undertaking was supported by IFAD's Executive Board and Management, who were open to engaging with IOE throughout the evaluation process, sharing necessary data, information and documentation.

The effort was supported by a team of consultants, with country case studies mostly done by national consultants, and two senior independent advisers, who ensured that IOE and its consultants followed the most appropriate evaluation methodology and process to conduct this evaluation, and who also reviewed and commented on several deliverables, including the draft final report.

Emerging evaluation findings were discussed with IFAD Management in a timely manner, both informally and formally. Management was given the opportunity to review and comment on the emerging findings in an interim report, and their feedback was duly considered by IOE in the preparation of the draft final evaluation report, on which they also had a chance to comment. The main findings were presented to the Evaluation Committee and the Executive Board for their feedback before the preparation of the final evaluation report.

Overview. The CLEE found that a number of initiatives to enhance efficiency and effectiveness had been undertaken in recent years and while the evaluation was underway. Efficiency initiatives included the introduction of direct supervision and implementation support, expanded country presence, the Change and Reform Agenda, commitments related to efficiency undertaken in the context of Ninth Replenishment of IFAD's Resources consultations, a more transparent and strengthened budget process, and the even more recent Strategic Workforce Plan.

On the operational front, IFAD was engaged in a fundamental transition from a focus on financing individual projects to a programmatic approach linking knowledge, policy dialogue and partnerships to projects in each country, and with growing attention to the scaling-up agenda.

IOE was aware that it would take time for the full benefits of many management decisions and reforms to be fully realized. At the same time, it found a number of opportunities for increased efficiency at different levels, although it reminded Management and the Executive Board that there were likely to be trade-offs.

With respect to the governing bodies, the CLEE found that their overall architecture was complex, but worked. The non-resident nature of the Board was seen as a positive characteristic but also contributed to an overloaded agenda. There were opportunities for the Governing Council to delegate to the Executive Board, and for the Board to delegate to Management. The evaluation report included a dedicated chapter on the efficiency of IFAD governing bodies, with many interesting findings to be considered.

Recommendations. The overarching recommendation was that IFAD 'raise the bar for IFAD's own performance as a partner to promote scaled-up impact' of the operations it supported, aspiring to deliver 'satisfactory or better' performance, against the observed practice of 'moderately satisfactory or better'. This recommendation was grounded in the rationale that, for IFAD to make a significant impact, it had to leverage its resources by attracting partner resources on a very large scale in order to replicate and scale up pioneering, innovative IFAD-funded operations and activities.

This point was supported by seven sub-recommendations:

- Aim for scaling up of high-impact, innovative approaches emerging from IFAD-supported projects and programmes, which should become the objective of IFAD's business model.
- Articulate and implement a clear vision for country presence and how IFAD would operate in a decentralized environment.
- Manage oversight and support units, including critical ICT functions, with a clear focus on increasing service quality and cost efficiency.
- Better manage scarce budgetary resources towards high-quality results.
- Strategically manage the skills, cost and performance of the workforce.
- Focus oversight by the governing bodies on key strategic issues, with more attention to discussing results, lessons and evaluations.
- Instill an institutional culture of accountability and performance, and strengthen the reporting for results.

With respect to the governing bodies, the evaluation also recommended introducing a code of conduct, a normal feature of IFIs, and developing broad terms of reference for Executive Board members to assist Member States in designating their representatives.

Discussions of the CLEE by the Evaluation Committee and the Executive Board resulted in broad agreement on the recommendations, and highlighted the critical importance of effective and timely follow-up. Management and IOE agreed that the best way forward was to combine the recommendations of the evaluation and the efficiency-related commitments undertaken in IFAD9 consultations into a single, consolidated action plan to further enhance IFAD's efficiency.

Actions. Among the many actions taken in response to the CLEE, a number of initiatives were taken to improve resource management in IFAD. The Fund's performance management process was further enhanced, and a reward-and-recognition framework was adopted, including monetary and non-monetary rewards.

Additionally, a new competency framework was launched in support of staff recruitment, development and performance management, and also aimed to contribute to staff motivation and performance.

IFAD's Engagement in Fragile and Conflict-affected States and Situations (2015)[10]

In December 2016, IFAD presented a new strategy for engagement in countries with fragile situations. The Organization's new approach grew to a great extent out of a CLE conducted on this issue in 2014/2015. The evaluation explored IFAD's work over a ten-year period, from 2004 until the end of 2013.

IFAD's operations focus on rural poverty reduction, rural development and transformation, rather than fragility per se. However, a situation of fragility can influence the opportunities and constraints which IFAD faces at the operational and strategic levels, just as contributing to rural development may improve a fragile situation, particularly if localized. Agenda 2030 has recognized addressing fragility as one of the 'six essential elements' required for delivery of the SDGs.

Evaluation challenges. One of the constraints faced by this evaluation was the absence of a common international classification of fragile countries and situations. Also, IFAD did not have a unified policy document dealing with fragility. The definition of fragility was formulated in 2006, applied to fragile states (but not fragile sub-national situations within states classified as non-fragile) and had not been revisited since then. As a result, the definition did not adequately reflect recent policy debates (e.g. key principles stemming from the Busan Partnership Agreement, which offers an international framework for dialogue and actions to enhance the effectiveness of cooperation in support of international development).

Another challenge was to conceptualize and capture the linkages between IFAD's work and fragile states and situations. To address this issue, the evaluation prepared a schematic results chain. For each step in the results chain, key assumptions were identified. Although it did not correspond to a fully-fledged TOC, it made explicit the tacit approach to fragility delineated in several IFAD documents and constituted a useful structure for the evaluative enquiry. The results chain highlighted the importance of IFAD's strategy and project design responding to the country's fragility; the nature of project design and implementation support; and outcomes that reflect the needs of a fragile state or situation. Each of these was examined during the evaluation.(See Figure 3.2.)

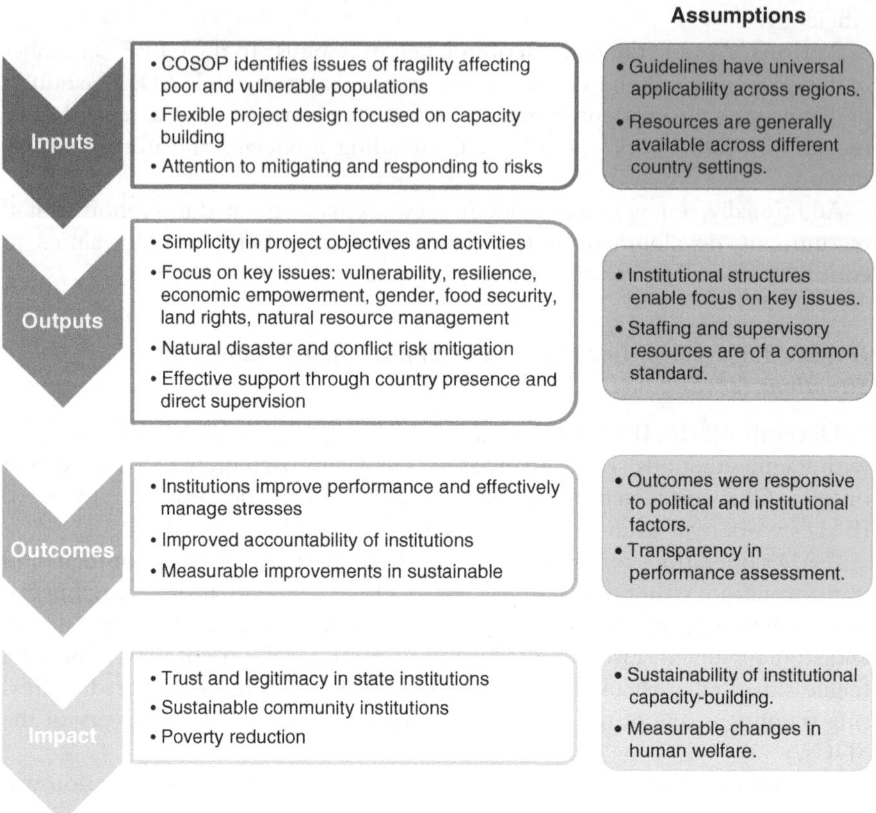

Figure 3.2 Notional results chain for IFAD's engagement with fragile states.*

* The results chain draws on the approach taken by the Independent Evaluation Group at the World Bank in the 2013 Evaluation of International Development Association's support to Fragile States (World Bank, 2013).

Source: International Fund for Agricultural Development (IFAD) (2015).

Findings. The evaluation found that the performance of IFAD-funded projects in countries that had always been classified as fragile was lower than in countries that had moved in and out of fragility, or that had never been classified as fragile. However, there were significant improvements in countries that had always been fragile in terms of overall project achievement, project effectiveness, IFAD's performance as a partner, and rural poverty impact.

Achievements in promoting GEWE had not improved in countries that had always been fragile, whereas they showed improvement in countries which were only partially or never fragile.

The evaluation pinpointed some of the key explanatory factors for weaker performance.

- The context analyses in strategic and project documents did not sufficiently examine drivers of fragility. This resulted in over-ambitious objectives and complex project designs, adding an additional stress factor to an already constrained institutional capacity.
- There was a limited availability of skills among (and available training for) staff working in fragile situations. Also, budgets for analytical work, design, supervision, implementation support and self-evaluation were not adequate for situations of fragility.
- There were extreme weaknesses in data-collection systems, low capacity for analysis and insufficient resources for activities that are not always seen as priorities, especially under conflict and crisis circumstances.
- Procurement systems, financial management and auditing were weak, with major overruns in project management costs (in some cases, close to 50 per cent of total project costs).
- Although IFAD had several corporate guidance documents on topics related to fragile states, post-conflict and disaster early recovery, there was no single overarching policy statement that could serve as the main reference for IFAD staff and consultants, or clarify to Member States and other development partners the Organization's role and priorities in this area. Moreover, the existing documents did not provide sufficient clarity on definitions, did not consider the wider issues of fragility and conflict, and contained limited explanation of the differences between conflict, conflict prevention, post-conflict rehabilitation and transitional development.

Recommendations. The CLE made recommendations regarding policy and strategy, project and programme design and implementation, staff development and IFAD's results measurement framework. Below are some of the recommendations.

- <u>Policy and strategy</u>. Draft an overarching corporate policy statement for approval by the Executive Board, including a new definition that would set out the principles for IFAD's approach to engagement with fragile and conflict-affected states and sub-national situations. As part of the policy, clearly define the development threshold that would assist staff in determining the fragility situation in particular countries or regions, allowing them to design operations using appropriate tools and instruments.
- <u>Project and programme design</u>. Programme design would need to identify where IFAD could engage and where it could not. In countries with sub-national fragile situations, where basic security requirements did not preclude IFAD's involvement, IFAD would need to decide whether to engage based on the potential for impact on rural poverty.
- <u>Project and programme implementation</u>. Expand direct supervision and implementation support in quantity and technical content, ensuring allocation of corresponding budgets based on needs rather than on pre-determined allocations by project. It was recommended that technical

staff from IFAD's Policy and Technical Advisory Division further expand their participation in such processes as well as in COSOP and project designs.

- Staff development. Introduce specific incentives for staff working in fragile states and conflict-affected situations, including those based in headquarters discharging similar functions. Include working in fragile situations as a main criterion for professional development and diversification as well as career advancement within the broader framework of IFAD's performance evaluation system.
- IFAD's results measurement framework. Revise the framework to include indicators of outcomes related to fragility. The major gaps lay in measuring women's empowerment and institutional performance.

Actions. This evaluation was followed by an approach paper for IFAD's strategy for engagement in countries with fragile situations, presented to the Evaluation Committee in March 2016, and the Executive Board the following month. Following feedback, the final strategy was prepared as part of a corporate paper addressing fragility, MICs, the PBAS and decentralization.

IOE pointed out some issues which warranted further consideration, as Management moved towards its final strategy. These were related to: policy coherence; resource allocation; M&E; differentiated allocation of the administrative budget; strengthening learning loops; and gender mainstreaming.

In the thirteenth edition of PRISMA, issued in August 2016, Management indicated that IOE's recommendations and comments had either been addressed or were under ongoing consideration, as IFAD moved towards a final strategy, which was included in a corporate paper submitted in December 2016 addressing fragility, MICs, PBAS and decentralization.

In order to implement this new strategy, IFAD will develop further guidelines and/or update existing ones. All guidelines will be developed/updated by the end of 2017. The strategy will inform operations through the remaining period of the Tenth Replenishment of IFAD's Resources (IFAD10) (until the end of 2018) and IFAD11 (2019–2021), with a review to be conducted as part of the IFAD11 Midterm Review.

IFAD's Decentralization Experience (2016)[11]

In 2016, IOE conducted a CLE on IFAD's experience with decentralization, covering the period from 2003 through mid-2016 and including notes gathered from comparator organizations. The evaluation was instrumental in the preparation of a corporate decentralization plan that IFAD Management presented to the Executive Board in December 2016.

The evaluation was undertaken within the framework of the IFAD Evaluation Policy and followed the methodological principles set out in the second edition of the Evaluation Manual. It was conducted in keeping with the internationally recognized criteria of relevance, effectiveness and efficiency.

More specifically, the CLE was designed to assess and generate learning to strengthen future strategies and plans in the following areas:

- IFAD's decentralization experience and efforts;
- The contribution of IFAD decentralization to improved operational performance and to achieving better development results;
- The costs of the decentralization process in relation to the results achieved.

Background. When it began operations in 1978, IFAD's original intention was to work through existing international organizations, rather than operate its own country offices, but over the years the Fund's approach to working with countries changed. In 2003, the Executive Board approved the Field Presence Pilot Programme, leading to the establishment of 15 country offices. In 2011, the Board approved the IFAD Country Presence Policy and Strategy and set a cap of 40 country offices. Later, that figure was raised to 50 (International Fund for Agricultural Development, 2017).

IFAD's country presence has included four major configurations. The first was based on a national staff member-country programme officer leading the office under the supervision of an international staff member based in Rome. The second was based on an international staff member-country programme manager out-posted in a country and supported by national staff.

The third configuration to emerge was a sub-regional office led by an international staff member, providing services to neighbouring countries as well. The fourth was that of a regional office – established only in Kenya – led by an international staff member and with some decentralized financial functions covering the East and Southern Africa region and part of the West and Central Africa region.

Findings. The evaluation found that, through its country presence, IFAD has improved its understanding of the national development context and its capacity to provide timely and responsive implementation support to its operations. In turn, this enhanced capacity has contributed to better development results in areas including on-the-ground impact, gender equality, sustainability of benefits, innovation and scaling up.

Additionally, country presence has been instrumental to improving partnerships with governmental actors and international donors, although it has contributed less than expected to knowledge management and policy dialogue, partly due to limited human and financial resources. The evaluation also found that engagement in policy dialogue largely depended on the relevant interests and experience of individual staff members.

Challenges to decentralization. The evaluation also found that one of the main challenges to the decentralization process would be to strike a balance between operational efficiency and cost-sensitive approaches, with the need to deepen and strengthen country presence.

The evaluation noted that the Organization could have benefited to a greater extent from information available from previous evaluations and the experiences of other organizations. A wide range of expected objectives were found to be mismatched with the limited staff and financial resources. Also, greater focus was placed on expanding country presence than on reorganizing/adjusting resources at headquarters, the latter also being an important part of the decentralization process.

Recommendations. The evaluation recommended consolidating IFAD's country presence while enhancing cost efficiency and implementing a plan to reduce staff at headquarters, while increasing staff working near the country programmes. The evaluation also recommended increasing support for non-lending activities, differentiating the non-lending agenda according to the type of country office and its resource capacity, and establishing a dedicated budget line. In addition it recommended improvements in the following areas: delegation of authority to country directors and training; staff incentives and capacity to operate in a decentralized environment; and the quality of data, monitoring and self-assessment.

F. African Development Bank (AfDB)–IFAD Joint Evaluation on Agriculture and Rural Development in Africa (2010)[12]

The AfDB–IFAD joint evaluation 'Towards purposeful partnerships in African agriculture' was the first joint evaluation between the two organizations to review relevant development policies and operations of AfDB and IFAD in Africa. The evaluation set the stage for a more synergistic approach across the organizations to evaluating agriculture and rural development. It also established the basis on which IOE would develop good practices for future joint evaluations.

The evaluation had four objectives: (i) to determine the relevance of agriculture and rural development policies and operations, in the light of current and emerging issues; (ii) to assess the performance and impact of the two organizations; (iii) to evaluate the strategic partnership between IFAD and AfDB and other agriculture and rural development partnerships on the continent; and (iv) to develop recommendations to enhance the partnership and development effectiveness of the two institutions.

Attention was devoted to analysing the changing context of agriculture and rural development in Africa, and to drawing out the relevant strategic implications. The evaluation found that although the economic situation had improved in many parts of Africa in recent years, and although sector policies had improved, many challenges remained, including: poor infrastructure; weak sector institutions and insufficient regional integration; underdeveloped markets and limited private sector involvement; low productivity of smallholder farmers; the need for effective management of natural resources and the environment, in the face of climate change; high levels of poverty, exacerbated by rapid population growth and the continued prevalence of HIV/AIDS; difficult access to both domestic and international markets, which constrains production; and pervasive gender inequality, which undercuts the contribution of women in a region where they play key roles in agriculture and agricultural trade.

Actions required to address these challenges include: improving the investment climate; strengthening infrastructure and regional integration; supporting innovation; and developing institutional capacity. However, the African context in all dimensions is complex and highly diverse, and solutions need to be tailored to fit local conditions. The country context is key.

Notes

1 International Fund for Agricultural Development (IFAD) (2002a).
2 International Fund for Agricultural Development (IFAD) (2003).
3 IFAD (2005).
4 International Fund for Agricultural Development (IFAD) (2002b).
5 International Fund for Agricultural Development (IFAD) (2010a).
6 International Fund for Agricultural Development (IFAD) (2005a).
7 International Fund for Agricultural Development (IFAD) (2007).
8 International Fund for Agricultural Development (IFAD) (2010b).
9 International Fund for Agricultural Development (IFAD) (2013).
10 IFAD (2015).
11 International Fund for Agricultural Development (IFAD) (2016).
12 African Development Bank-IFAD (2010).

References

African Development Bank–IFAD. 2010. Joint Evaluation on Agriculture and Rural Development in Africa: Towards Purposeful Partnerships in African Agriculture. Rome: IFAD.

Caviezel, L., Dabelstein, N., Feinstein, O., Lombin, G., Khan, A.B., Morales Melendez, V.H. and van den Berg, R. 2002. External Review of the Results and Impact of IFAD Operations. External Review Team. Rome: IFAD.

Felloni, F., Garcia, O.A. and Muthoo, A.K. 2016. Evaluating IFAD's Support to Rural Development in Fragile States and Situations. Evaluation Connections. European Evaluation Society newsletter. April 2016, 12–13. Prague: EES.

Felloni, F., Muthoo, A.K. and Torralba, M. 2014. The Evaluation Experience of the International Fund for Agricultural Development (IFAD). *Revista de Evaluación de Programas y Políticas Públicas (Journal of Public Programs and Policy Evaluation* 3, 53–79). Madrid: Universidad Nacional de Educación a Distancia.

Garcia, O.A. 2015. Influential Evaluations: Illustrations from Multilateral Development Organizations. Evaluation Matters, First Quarter. Abidjan: African Development Bank, 22–26.

Højlund, S. 2014. Evaluation Use in Evaluation Systems: The Case of the European Commission. *Evaluation: The International Journal of Theory, Research and Practice* 20 (4), 428–432.

Independent External Evaluation of IFAD. 2004–2005. IFAD website: www.ifad.org/web/ioe/-/independent-external-evaluation-of-ifad-ie-5. Rome: IFAD.

Independent Evaluation Group. 2013. Evaluation of International Development Association's support to Fragile States. World Bank Group.

International Fund for Agricultural Development (IFAD). 2002a. External Review of the Results and Impact of IFAD Operations. Rome: IFAD.

International Fund for Agricultural Development (IFAD). 2002b. IFAD's Capacity as a Promoter of Replicable Innovations. Corporate-level Evaluation. Independent Office of Evaluation of IFAD. Rome: IFAD.

International Fund for Agricultural Development (IFAD). 2003. United Republic of Tanzania Country Portfolio Evaluation. Independent Office of Evaluation of IFAD. Rome: IFAD.

International Fund for Agricultural Development. 2005. IFAD's Action Plan to Increase Development Effectiveness. Rome: IFAD.

International Fund for Agricultural Development (IFAD). 2005a. Direct Supervision Pilot Programme. Corporate-level Evaluation. Independent Office of Evaluation of IFAD. Rome: IFAD.

International Fund for Agricultural Development (IFAD). 2005b. Independent External Evaluation of IFAD. Rome: IFAD.

International Fund for Agricultural Development (IFAD). 2007. Evaluation of IFAD's Field Presence Pilot Programme. Independent Office of Evaluation of IFAD. Rome: IFAD.

International Fund for Agricultural Development (IFAD). 2010a. IFAD's Capacity to Promote Innovation and Scaling Up. Corporate-level Evaluation. Independent Office of Evaluation of IFAD. Rome: Italy.

International Fund for Agricultural Development (IFAD). 2010b. IFAD's Performance with Regard to Gender Equality and Women's Empowerment. Corporate-level Evaluation. Independent Office of Evaluation of IFAD. Rome: IFAD.

International Fund for Agricultural Development (IFAD). 2013. IFAD's Institutional Efficiency and Efficiency of IFAD-funded Operations. Corporate-level Evaluation. Independent Office of Evaluation of IFAD. Rome: IFAD.

International Fund for Agricultural Development (IFAD). 2015. IFAD's Engagement in Fragile and Conflict-affected States and Situations. Corporate-level Evaluation. Independent Office of Evaluation of IFAD. Rome: IFAD.

International Fund for Agricultural Development (IFAD). 2016. IFAD's Decentralization Experience. Corporate-level Evaluation. Independent Office of Evaluation of IFAD. Rome: IFAD.

International Fund for Agricultural Development (IFAD). 2017. IFAD's Support to Scaling up of Results. Evaluation Synthesis. Independent Office of Evaluation of IFAD. Rome: IFAD.

Levington, L.C. 2003. Evaluation Use: Advances, Challenges and Applications. *American Journal of Evaluation* 24(4), 525–535.

4 Evaluations of Inclusive Development

In the 2030 Agenda for Sustainable Development, Member States recognize that eradicating poverty in all its forms and dimensions is the greatest global challenge and an indispensable requirement for sustainable development. In committing to the realization of the 2030 Agenda they also attempt to leave no one behind – notably people from marginalized groups. This chapter will illustrate highlights and learning from evaluations related to gender equality and women's empowerment (GEWE), indigenous peoples, pastoralists and young people.

A. Evaluation and Gender Mainstreaming

Influential evaluations, coupled with IFAD's evolving Evaluation Policy and Evaluation Manual, have contributed to shaping the Fund's design and performance of poverty-reduction interventions, as well as overall shifts in organizational structure and focus. One noteworthy example of this is IFAD's focus on GEWE.

The introduction of specific, gender-related criteria and indicators in IFAD's Evaluation Manual, together with pivotal evaluations, contributed to IFAD's adoption, in 2012, of a gender policy, and have continued to influence the formulation of relevant projects and evaluations.

IFAD has increasingly made overcoming gender inequalities and empowering women a cornerstone of its work to reduce rural poverty and food insecurity. In the early 2000s, the IFAD Strategic Framework (2002–2006) recognized that rural poverty reduction was intrinsically linked to women's empowerment and gender equality, and IFAD developed the Gender Plan of Action for implementation between 2003 and 2006. The action plan's overall objective was to systematize and scale up ongoing efforts to mainstream a gender perspective in different aspects of IFAD's work and to comply with the many United Nations commitments.

As previously discussed, the 2009/10 peer review by the ECG, 'Peer Review of IFAD's Office of Evaluation and Evaluation Function', led to a number of changes to IFAD's evaluation system. These changes were incorporated into the Fund's revised Evaluation Policy. By that time, the Evaluation Manual explicitly mentioned GEWE as performance criteria to be considered in the newly designated CSPEs.

The peer review roughly coincided with the IOE CLE entitled 'IFAD's performance with regard to Gender Equality and Women's Empowerment', which began in 2009. The CLE recommended that IFAD develop an evidence- and results-based corporate policy on GEWE for submission to the Executive Board in 2011. The policy would be IFAD's principal reference document on this area of focus, bringing under one umbrella the Fund's main related strategic objectives and priorities. The recommended policy would also need to indicate how key corporate business processes would be adjusted for better results on the ground. Additionally, the CLE recommended that IFAD Management conduct a dedicated, comprehensive review of the Organization's overall gender architecture, to ensure that IFAD had adequate human resources and funds to achieve the desired results in borrowing countries. (See Figure 4.1).

Moreover, the evaluation recommended that GEWE be included as one of the 'big bets' in IFAD's corporate innovation agenda until 2015, and that IFAD remain open to promoting gender-related innovations at the country or project level which respond to context-specific challenges. COSOPs and project designs were to outline the specific efforts needed to ensure

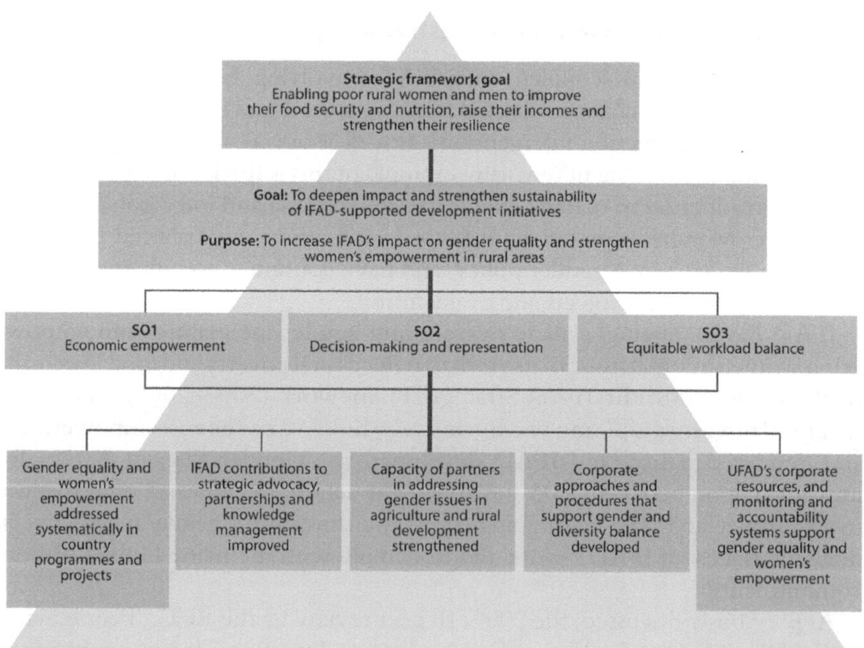

Note: SO= strategic objective.

Figure 4.1 Main elements of policy on gender equality and women's empowerment.

Source: IFAD Policy for Gender Equality and Women's Empowerment. September 2012.

that successful innovations could actually be scaled up for wider impact on GEWE.

Studying the Relationship of Women's Human and Social Capital and the Nutritional Status of Children

Between 1999 and 2001, IOE (then the 'Office of Evaluation and Studies') conducted household surveys in Nepal and in Papua New Guinea to study the relationship of women's human and social capital and nutritional status of children up to five years old. The results of these surveys, as well as the use of anthropometric data as an indicator of children's and households' well-being, were discussed at an international workshop organized by IFAD in Fiuggi (Italy) in September 2011.

Do Empowered Rural Women's Organizations in Nepal and Papua New Guinea Address Child Undernutrition?

By Per A. Eklund, former IOE Senior Evaluation Officer, 1990–2001

Background. Poverty is still predominantly rural, and nested among those who practice agriculture for their livelihood. Moving out of agriculture is associated with reducing poverty[1] but little is known about how households escape from vulnerability when monetary poverty is combined with capability poverty, which is triggered by net deficits in dietary intake at an early age. Chronic child undernutrition, if not addressed before the age of two, presents the risk of impairing cognitive and motor abilities, reducing school achievement and physical work capacity, thus significantly lowering adult productivity and increasing susceptibility to disease.[2] Moreover, infants combatting infection when they are deprived of nutrients further restricts their physical stature and growth of brain neural circuits. Children are likely to pass from underweight to chronically malnourished, or stunted, when mothers are exposed to inter-seasonal episodes of nutrient deficiencies. These factors reduce the probability of entry into skills-intensive non-agricultural employment.

Capability poverty, with impaired brain development, perpetuates socio-economic disparities.[3] The World Bank president stated that ending extreme poverty by 2030 requires that children escape their parents' vulnerability and reach their mental development potential.[4] One quarter of children under five worldwide – 159 million – are stunted. The proportion in sub-Saharan Africa and South Asia exceeds 36 per cent. Even in countries that have done reasonably well in terms of economic growth, such as Ethiopia, Guatemala, India and Indonesia, over one third of children remain stunted. Food security, markets and economic growth alone are not sufficient solutions. A further prerequisite is empowering mothers in poor households with nutrition knowledge. Poverty measures based on income or expenditure data obtained through household surveys neglect the non-monetary aspects of well-being, whereas child anthropometry indicators reflect net deficits in dietary intake at an early age.

Rural women's informal associations. Women's informal associations are found in most rural societies in developing countries. They have the potential to empower members to mobilize savings to smooth consumption, provide a buffer for unforeseen outlays for illness and emergencies, and facilitate cooperative solutions towards improved livelihood systems. Cohesive groups that improve women's status have been found to have a strong positive effect on the nutrition status of the women themselves and on caring practices for their children.[5] Evidence suggests that women who build their own associations do so based on shared values in rearing, nourishing and protecting their children; this translates into high levels of interpersonal trust, nurtured exchange, member participation and little tolerance for 'free riding'. In contrast, when external agents form entirely new groups, interpersonal trust and cooperative behaviour are not a foregone conclusion.

Informal rural women's organizations in Nepal and Papua New Guinea. With endemic rural poverty and poor governance prevalent in Nepal and Papua New Guinea (PNG) towards the end of the 1990s, IOE conducted studies to explore whether participation in informal mutual support associations can reduce children's undernutrition. The results of these studies, comprised primarily of household surveys, as well as the use of anthropometric data as an indicator of children's and households' well-being, were discussed at an international workshop organized by IFAD in Fiuggi, Italy in September 2011.

The hypothesis tested was that child malnutrition is lower for community-based organizations (CBOs) with a higher degree of capabilities. The derived composite maturity index reflected eight dimensions of organizational effectiveness and the degree of autonomy of the CBO.

Does social capital, measured by the maturity index of women's organizations, contribute to reducing prevalence of child malnutrition? The studies in Nepal and PNG explored interactions between women-based CBOs and the nutritional status of children under five in the most deprived member households.[6,7] Would different activities undertaken by CBOs, separately or aggregated, generate an improved nutritional status in children under five? The proxy for vulnerability, for non-income poverty, was the prevalence of malnutrition, with anthropometric indicators, for children less than five years of age.

In Nepal, the 1999 survey comprised 63 CBOs and 427 households. In PNG, the 2000 survey comprised 67 CBOs and 310 households. Three different types of CBOs were surveyed. In Nepal, traditional Mothers' Groups, not receiving any support for their activities, were compared with

UNICEF-supported CBOs and with CBOs supported by government programmes and IFAD's Production Credit for Rural Women without any growth promotion or nutrition education. (In the UNICEF-supported programme, female facilitators supported growth monitoring combined with nutrition education.) In PNG, traditional Mothers' Groups, not receiving any support for their activities for their members, were compared with CBOs supported by IFAD's Northern Simbu Development Project and by church groups. (For background see IFAD country programme evaluations).[8,9]

Key Findings

The cooperative behaviour of Mothers' Groups that are not externally supported reduces child underweight, with the risk of transition to stunting. The more capable Mothers' Groups are in Nepal and PNG, the lower the level of underweight of members' children under five. For externally supported groups, the maturity index does not have any significant effects associated with less malnutrition (underweight and stunting) of children.

Raising mothers' knowledge about stunting, determinants and children's risk of impaired livelihood prospects is essential. Interventions to raise maternal nutrition knowledge significantly accelerate progress in addressing child undernutrition across CBOs, promising substantial longer-term impact. In PNG, training contributed to reduced child underweight. In Nepal, **community development interventions were effective** in reducing stunting when they were combined with out-of-school learning. Knowledge of nutrition determinants also generates interventions designed to reduce infection. For example, improved drinking water (through hand pumps) improved the nutritional status of very young children (Nepal), whereas in PNG, diarrhoea worsened stunting and underweight. The results also suggest that availability of relevant information on nutrition and child growth from radio is an effective instrument with which to reinforce the training provided by village facilitators. Additional studies, e.g.in Ethiopia and Morocco,[10,11] confirm the importance of raised maternal nutrition knowledge.

Clearly, supporting autonomous rural women's associations (particularly through nutrition education) with a view to addressing long-term capability poverty and associated chronic child undernutrition is key to enabling the next generation to escape their parents' vulnerability and engage in productive farm and non-farm employment.

1 Dercon, S. 2006. 'Risk, Growth and Poverty', presented at the conference 'Frontiers in practice: Reducing poverty through better diagnostics', March 2006, Washington, D.C.

2 World Bank. 2006. Directions in Development, Repositioning Nutrition as Central to Development, A Strategy for Large Scale Action, Washington, D.C.
3 Eklund, P. 2014. Capability poverty by net deficits in dietary intake at early age - neglected by the Rangarajan Poverty line, Indian J Community Health, Supp. 1, November 2014, ISSN 2248–9509.
4 Kim Jim Yong. www.worldbank.org/en/news/speech/2016/04/14/remarks-world-bank-group-president-Jim-yong-Kim-early-childhood-development.
5 Smith, L. C, Ramakrishnan U., Ndiaye A, Haddad L. and Martorell R. 2003. 'The Importance of Women's Status for Child Nutrition in Developing Countries.' Research Report 131. Washington, D.C.: IFPRI.
6 Eklund, P., Felloni, F. and Imai, K. Women's Organisations, Maternal Knowledge, and Social Capital to Reduce Prevalence of Stunted Children – Evidence from Rural Nepal. *Journal of Development Studies*. 2007.
7 Imai, K. and Eklund, P. Women's Organizations and Social Capital to Reduce Prevalence of Child Malnutrition in Papua New Guinea. *Oxford Development Studies* 36(2): 209–233. DOI: 10.1080/13600810701701996.
8 Country Programme Evaluation Nepal, IFAD, Rome, 1999.
9 Country Programme Evaluation Papua and New Guinea, IFAD, Rome, 2002.
10 Christiaensen, L. and Alderman, H. 2001. 'Child Malnutrition in Ethiopia: Can Maternal Knowledge Augment the Role of Income', World Bank Africa Region Working Paper Series, No. 22, October 2001, Washington, D.C.
11 Glewwe, P. 1999. Why Does Mother's Schooling Raise Child Health in Developing Countries: Evidence from Morocco. *Journal of Human Resources* 34(1): 124–159.

Evaluation Synthesis on Gender[1]

IFAD has committed to improving its performance on gender practices during the period of the Tenth Replenishment of IFAD's Resources (IFAD10), in particular the share of GEWE interventions aiming at transformative change.

In this context, in 2017, IOE published an evaluation synthesis report on what works for GEWE – a review of practices and results (International Fund for Agricultural Development, 2017). The report highlights that there is no agreed definition of transformative change in IFAD, nor has the concept been operationalized in IFAD's work on gender yet. For the purpose of the evaluation synthesis, transformative approaches are defined as those that aim to overcome the root causes of inequality and discrimination through promoting sustainable, inclusive and far-reaching social change. Transformative approaches challenge existing social norms and the distribution of power and resources.

The report provides a conceptual framework in the form of a TOC that can be used to identify different types of practices and how they contribute to transformative processes. A TOC appropriately captures the nature of transformative change, for which results often take time to emerge.

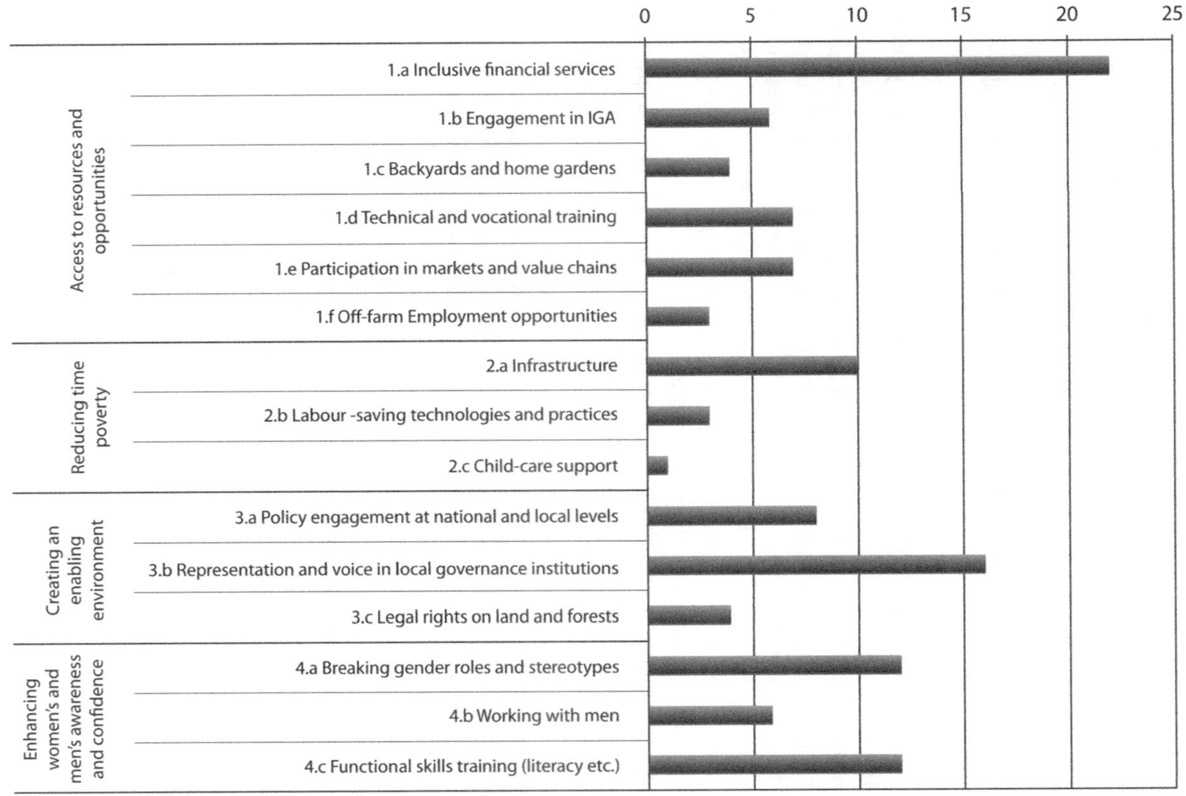

Chart 4.1 Number of GEWE practices in the sample classed by categories and areas

Source: Evaluation synthesis on 'What works for gender equality and women's empowerment – a review of practices and results'. International Fund for Agricultural Development (IFAD) (2017); IFAD website, (n.d.)

Thus, evaluations that typically take place sometime after project completion are in a position to assess whether gender norms, roles and relations have indeed been transformed.

The report provides a systematic review of gender-transformative practices and results documented in IOE evaluations since 2011. Within the sample of 57 evaluations, the synthesis identified 121 GEWE practices. Based on the four main practice areas of the TOC, the practices were classified into four main types:

(a) Improving women's access to resources and opportunities (47 practices or 39 per cent);
(b) Reducing women's time poverty (14 practices or 12 per cent);
(c) Addressing political, legal and institutional constraints (29 practices or 24 per cent); and
(d) Strengthening women's and men's awareness, consciousness and confidence (30 practices or 25 per cent).

Chart 4.1 provides an overview of the practice areas and the specific types of GEWE practices.

The review found that in many cases IFAD has supported transformative change by addressing root causes of gender inequality and women's powerlessness, in particular their exclusion from access to resources and opportunities and their limited social capital. But the report also highlights that policy engagement on gender, although a critical element to support transformative change, has not yet received sufficient attention.

The report contains a wealth of lessons and good practices. One important lesson is that transformation needs to be built into the design of projects. Interventions that had a clear transformative purpose were found to be more effective. This can include activities aiming to break traditional gender roles and stereotypes, but also strategies for social mobilization and leadership. Strategic alliances that include gender champions and agents of change, and networks between women's groups and activities, are important and should be more systematically pursued.

Based on the synthesis, the following guiding principles were identified:

(a) Practices that worked well, but are not yet common, should be promoted (e.g. value chains, marketing, off-farm employment).
(b) Labour-saving technologies and working with men are not common practices yet, but the available evidence suggests that they can be highly effective. Practices to influence men and traditional leaders and practices to address women's 'time poverty' should be widely integrated into IFAD's interventions.
(c) Practices that are common, but so far have yielded mixed results, should be improved based on the available international practices. IFAD should critically review some commonly held beliefs and assumptions about gendered

benefits and promote services that are better tailored to the strategic needs of women (e.g. inclusive rural finance, infrastructure, functional skills training).

(d) Some practices are highly relevant, but not yet effective or common (e.g. promotion of income-generating activities, land rights), often because they are meeting contextual limitations (social and cultural values, institutional and legal frameworks). For these practices, the assumptions and influencing factors (in their theories of change) that have been limiting their effectiveness and wider application need to be carefully reviewed. Wider application of the practices needs to be accompanied by adequate strategies to address the systemic issues that may limit their effectiveness.

(e) Policy engagement and scaling up successful (GEWE practices are key to enabling transformative change. There are some good practices already, but they need to be more widely understood and applied within IFAD.

(f) Finally, it is the combination of practices that brings about transformative change. Therefore, IFAD interventions should be encouraged to use a range of different practices that more comprehensively address the complexity of issues and factors affecting GEWE.

The recommendations from this report emphasize the need for IFAD to sharpen its understanding of and practices on gender throughout the programming cycle, from design to evaluation, for greater focus on gender-transformative results.

The report also includes an appendix of 20 examples of GEWE practices that were written up as case studies. The case studies help to better understand why certain practices have worked (or not worked) and provide excellent illustrations and a good opportunity for sharing lessons learned. The following is an extract from the case study on a Rwanda project illustrating findings from the 2012 Rwanda Country Programme Evaluation.

Rwanda Rural Small and Microenterprise Promotion Project, phase II

Case Study

In 2014,* Rwanda ranked 7 out of 142 countries in the Global Gender Gap index with a score of 0.785 (ranking 25 in economic participation, 6 in political empowerment, 118 in health and survival, and 114 in educational attainment). Further, while gender gaps are low in the economic sphere, the level of poverty of women and men is high. In rural areas and in agriculture, women play a particularly important role but need access to resources, inputs and markets. The 2012 Rwanda Country Programme Evaluation observes that 27 per cent of households in Rwanda are headed by women, and these households are not only vulnerable to poverty, but also to exploitation.

The project was designed to deal with the most vulnerable, which in the context of Rwanda included women, women-headed households, and households headed by children and orphans. The gender focus was therefore strong from the outset. The project aimed in particular to provide off-farm income opportunities and group leadership positions to women, particularly among women-/child-headed households and orphans. Participatory approaches were applied to communities recovering from conflict and to local government structures for the purpose of social reconstruction and enhanced cohesion.

The project sought to create value chains in coffee and to brand the coffee of women producers 'cafés des femmes', and link it to the fair trade market. Project components were capacity-building, support to rural small and medium enterprises and support to microfinance institutions.

Output: The 2012 CPE observes that women made up more than half of the apprentices trained in management, marketing and accounting related to enterprises in the project.

Impact: Microenterprise interventions have reached out to poor rural women and expanded their access to markets and increased their income. Linkages were made between women coffee producers and fair trade organizations and gourmet markets for organic coffee. Café des femmes fetched a high price on the market. Women coffee producers' income increased (no data provided).

Overall, the project has strengthened human capacity through community mobilization, literacy training, and skills transfer, with the objectives to open up additional off-farm income opportunities for the target group, develop functional businesses (microenterprises and cooperatives) and skills development capacities in rural areas (service providers). Capacities were developed within the public sector to transfer technologies, business skills, and start-up capital to microenterprises including economic common interest groups and cooperatives. Capacity-building efforts also targeted private sector operators (individuals and groups) involved in offering apprenticeships and business training. As such, individuals and group leaders were both the main recipients and the main providers of capacity-building efforts. More importantly, the project contributed to changing people's mindset to be more business-oriented. They are able to recognize opportunities and to develop strategies to start a business or to improve and further develop existing ones. Women and youth have greatly benefited from these advances. Particularly good progress was achieved in the mobilization and operation of microenterprises and cooperatives, although to date few have reached self-sufficiency. The project's impact on social cohesion is undeniable.

Success factors: The key success factors were investing in apprenticeship training, microfinance and organizing women. The high economic participation and decision-making of women to begin with may be a contributing factor ['may be' a contributing factor? I would think this was one of the key success factors]. The project achieved near parity in women's participation as a result of mainstreaming gender considerations in all aspects of project design and implementation. At design, it was anticipated that 30 per cent of the project beneficiaries would be women, but this target was surpassed to 50 per cent.

Limitations. The project focused almost exclusively on the collection of physical output data, while impact monitoring received little to no attention (owing to a weak M&E system), making it difficult to evaluate performance. The 2012 CPE noted that the reduction in women's workload was prioritized in some projects but not others; in the Rwandan context, more work is needed in this area.

* Data for 2011 to 2013 was not available for Rwanda.

B. Evaluation and Indigenous Peoples

In 2015, IFAD hosted the second global Indigenous Peoples' Forum, which institutionalized IFAD's consultation and dialogue with indigenous peoples' representatives at the national, regional and international levels. On that occasion, the forum focused on food systems and sustainable livelihoods, providing an opportunity for indigenous peoples and IFAD staff to analyse and learn from previous experiences, while strengthening their collaboration for rural transformation.

The agenda included a presentation and plenary discussion on the key emerging findings of the Evaluation Synthesis Report on IFAD's Engagement with Indigenous Peoples,[2] which was prepared by IOE.

The key areas reviewed included targeting approaches, indigenous peoples' participation in projects and strategy development, empowerment, and support to policy engagement and advocacy. The emerging findings indicated that considerable effort and progress had been made at the global level in terms of policy engagement and partnership development.

At country/project level, notable contributions had been made in some projects and countries (for example, access to land, empowerment, and influence on institutions and policies). However, it was pointed out that, in general, there is still room to further strengthen IFAD's engagement with indigenous peoples and its impact on the ground.

Among the issues put forward for reflection were the need for good diagnostic analysis in the country strategy-preparation stage and in project design, the importance of improved M&E at the project level, with disaggregated data and indicators relevant to indigenous peoples, and the need to enhance IFAD operational staff's understanding of indigenous peoples' issues. IOE also noted the need to enhance supervision and implementation support to projects with appropriate expertise.

C. Evaluation and Pastoral Development

Drylands represent 40 per cent of the planet's total land mass and are inhabited by some 2.5 billion people, including 40 per cent of Africans, 39 per cent of Asians and 30 per cent of South Americans. The exact number of pastoralists is unknown but estimates range from 50 million to 200 million worldwide. The highest concentration of vulnerable rural people is believed to live in the drylands.

For most of the history of pastoral development, pastoral systems have been looked at through the wrong lens. The foundational knowledge of pastoral development saw a U-turn some 20 years ago, following the revision of the main explanatory model in ecology. Decades of interventions based on incorrect assumptions have left a problematic, if unintentional, legacy of distortions, misunderstanding and invisibility that must be acknowledged today when engaging with pastoral systems. The key implication concerns the pastoralist use of mobility: in the drylands, variability in the spatial and temporal distribution of rains is reflected in the patterns in which nutrients accumulate and peak in the vegetation, a variability which is exploited by mobile herds.

In 2016, within the framework of the 'Statement of Intent' of 2 April 2013 for strengthening collaboration across the Rome-based development agencies, the evaluation offices of FAO and IFAD prepared a joint evaluation synthesis (JES) report on FAO's and IFAD's engagement in pastoral development.[3] The JES aimed to generate findings and recommendations to inform the design and implementation of ongoing and future policies, strategies and work in pastoral development of FAO and IFAD. The JES analysed projects and interventions carried out by both agencies between 2003 and 2013.

The report is structured to look first at the scientific understanding of pastoral systems and drylands, before turning to FAO's and IFAD's engagement in pastoral development. The analysis of the sample projects focuses on seven themes (poverty reduction, risk and vulnerability, institutions, gender equality, natural resources management, advocacy, and knowledge management). The report then looks at the wider lessons learned in pastoral development, before concluding with a storyline of the findings, strategic implications and recommendations.

The main evaluation findings were as follows:

- Rural poverty reduction is a fundamental goal for both agencies, and as such **pastoralism fits into the strategic planning of both IFAD and FAO**. They favour a systemic approach, see themselves as enablers of the rural poor, and commit to advocacy on their behalf. Both IFAD and FAO's national and international presence and track record as neutral, 'honest brokers' place them in an ideal position to fulfil this role. At the moment, **neither agency has a policy on engagement with pastoral development**. However, both agencies emphasize their commitment to targeting disadvantaged and excluded groups, especially in remote and neglected areas.
- From IFAD's **overall allocations** in loans and grants for the 2003–2013 period, the proportion that concerned the 31 pastoral-oriented projects in

the evaluation's comprehensive inventory was about 11 per cent. In the same period, FAO allocated funds to 163 projects in the comprehensive inventory, corresponding to 5 per cent of total allocated resources.

- **IFAD and FAO have carried out important and useful pastoral interventions on the ground**. The initial decision to engage in this area was backed by the full weight of the two organizations. They also engaged in a certain amount of advocacy on behalf of pastoralists. FAO's work on pastoral risk in Central Asia, especially Mongolia, reflected the new thinking about pastoralism. Much of IFAD's work on pastoral organizations and pasture tenure has reflected the changing perceptions of pastoralism. Occasionally, projects by IFAD, FAO and their partners have been at the forefront of thinking on pastoralism.
- **For most project evaluations, supporting 'pastoral and agro-pastoral communities' means supporting them in sedentary activities**, and there is usually no indication in the evaluations of how the project engaged with the objective of supporting pastoral livelihoods. Some evaluations offer valuable insights on the ways the projects did or did not engage with pastoral systems. However, as pastoralism is a small component in a larger project, such observations remain out of the recommendations or executive summary, which inevitably affects the learning process.
- **There have been some positive highlights in projects aimed at reducing poverty and hunger in and around pastoral settings**. This is especially true with regard to strengthening household economy following animal health interventions in FAO projects, and in community-based participatory approaches to institution-building in IFAD projects, used to identify and manage key resources and conflict. Evaluations praise the efforts of animal health inspection and certification for export, and the development of veterinary field services. In particular, the training of Community Animal Health Workers is consistently found to be effective in reaching pastoralists.

The JES recommendations were:

- **Develop a policy of engagement in pastoral development**. The new understanding of pastoral systems has not yet been fully translated into development practice, from project design to implementation and evaluation. A policy would be a useful way to guide the adaptation of new concepts of pastoralism to realities on the ground. The policy should not be developed in isolation and should stress coordination within and between the two agencies. The long-term economics of preventing and managing conflict, and avoiding encouraging unsustainable rural-to-urban migration, should be carefully considered.
- **Build and adapt capacity in FAO and IFAD**. Pastoral development interventions take place on the back of a problematic legacy. Misleading and counterproductive ideas from the past permeate the entire learning process. On the other hand, 'reading the context' correctly, learning and adapting are crucial to effectiveness and efficiency of impact. FAO's and

IFAD's capacities to achieve their goals with regard to pastoral systems need to be expanded and adapted. This includes developing a better understanding of pastoral systems, their operational logic, and their relation to dryland economies more generally. But it also includes the development of the capacity of desk and project staff to systematically track engagement with pastoral development and its management, including the format and conduct of evaluations and the composition of evaluation teams.

- **Manage key dimensions of risk**. Dimensions of risk need to be acknowledged and managed when engaging with drylands and pastoral development. The main adaptive livelihood and production strategy consists in harnessing variability as distinct from avoiding it. In engaging with pastoral development, IFAD and FAO should assume that such risks are the rule rather than the exception, and embed measures to manage them as standard practice at all levels of operation.
- **Support advocacy by pastoralists, and on behalf of pastoralists and people whose livelihoods depend on pastoral systems**. FAO's and IFAD's significant influence in the international and national arenas represents an invaluable asset in the ongoing global effort to update the public perception of drylands and pastoral systems and come to terms with the legacy of misunderstanding and technical exclusion that represents perhaps the biggest obstacle to the development of resilient livelihood systems in the drylands. Advocacy is a crucial complement in today's engagement with pastoral development, but care should be taken to keep it within a systemic approach, subject to critical scrutiny and carefully targeted in light of the new understanding of drylands and pastoralism.

D. Evaluation of Rural Youth Interventions

IFAD started enhancing its focus on rural youth in the last decade and particularly in 2010, when the Strategic Framework for the period 2011–2015 reflected the Fund's attention and commitment to promoting the development of rural youth. In 2014, IOE conducted an evaluation synthesis on rural youth.[4] Overall, among the projects selected for this evaluation, about 83 per cent of past pro-youth projects targeted rural youth explicitly and 42 per cent included youth-specific activities. The evaluation highlights that IFAD is equipped with ad-hoc strategies, policies and guidelines to work with rural youth. Looking forward, the evaluation offers a number of reflections for IFAD, to ensure that rural youth play a catalytic role in rural transformation and agricultural sustainability: mainstreaming youth across country programmes in all regions; investing in the update of the knowledge base on youth and adequate socio-economic profiling; resolving the issue of efficiency versus equity upfront at the design stage in terms of identifying target groups; adopting systematically age-disaggregated monitoring indicators, to foster IFAD's learning and replication processes; and enhancing strategic partnerships to support the scaling up of successful and innovative models.

The evaluation, which was mandated to find ways in which IFAD could improve its work with rural young people, first reviewed recent literature on youth development with a view to building an argument in favour of rural investments that benefit young people. It then assessed IFAD's past loans and grants and the work of other organizations to identify comparative advantages, lessons learned and partnership potential. In the context of the post-2015 agenda, the evaluation suggested five ways in which developing country partners could cultivate the potential of their young people.

(i) **Mainstream youth issues in country programmes.** IFAD has adopted this as a major principle of engagement in its Strategic Framework,[5] and established policies and guidelines to guide the design and implementation of country programmes with favourable outcomes for young people. The main challenge concerns the systematic integration of IFAD's knowledge into its operations and consistent application of its fifth principle of engagement (e.g. the creation of viable opportunities for rural youth), and providing financial support that is commensurate to the task envisaged.

(ii) **Invest in updating knowledge about youth issues and socio-economic profiles.** Both investments must influence project design and lead to improvements in the quality of response in country programmes to issues affecting young people. The information gathered will inform targeting strategies, support packages, project management and the sequencing of activities with a view to achieving outcomes that favour young people. IFAD must prioritize the allocation of resources to this updating of its knowledge base during socio-economic profiling at the project design stage. The justification is clear in that IFAD will increasingly be called to assist Member States classified as MICs with specialist information and trend analysis rather than with financial support.

(iii) **Resolve the issues of efficiency and equity in terms of identifying target groups.** A common question is: 'Which youth groups is the project targeting?' The heterogeneity of rural young people is a targeting challenge in itself; it is compounded by the need to balance design with the available management capacities and to focus on a few activities that will drive development and extend programme outreach to young people and particular youth groups. IFAD should adopt direct targeting of particular sub-groups on the basis of clear eligibility criteria rather than self-targeting approaches so that the risks of spreading resources too thinly and having to state what cannot be done are avoided. Evaluations noted that grouping young people with other vulnerable groups and implementing self-targeting approaches alone did not lead to success. The questions to be addressed are which organizations will target those left out of IFAD-funded projects, and to what extent IFAD can advocate on their behalf.

(iv) **Adopt age-disaggregated monitoring indicators to enable IFAD to learn, report results and support scaling up.** The adoption of age-disaggregated monitoring indicators for COSOPs and projects will enable

IFAD to learn what works and adjust its interventions accordingly, share its knowledge with partners, and evolve into an enabling platform for scaling up successful models.

Partnering is fundamental to IFAD's work with rural young people. Providing comprehensive assistance packages to young people calls for a range of skills, types of investment and resources that cannot be provided by IFAD and governments alone. Partnerships are therefore essential: they must be flexible and effective, and must enable IFAD to learn from its collaborators and develop innovative approaches. In this context, IFAD must determine whether grant-funded innovations and pilot initiatives for young people are adequately balanced with work in learning and scaling up, and ensure that procedures are in place for engaging with other actors such as private-sector organizations and South–South cooperation frameworks that can mobilize more resources than official development assistance. IFAD's successful intervention models now need to be scaled up to provide adequate responses to the needs of young populations. To achieve this, more IFAD investments will have to be combined with inputs from its humanitarian partners.

Notes

1 IFAD (2017).
2 International Fund for Agricultural Development (IFAD) (2015).
3 International Fund for Agricultural Development (IFAD) (2016a).
4 International Fund for Agricultural Development (IFAD) (2014).
5 International Fund for Agricultural Development (IFAD) (2016b).

References

International Fund for Agricultural Development (IFAD). IFAD website on gender: www.ifad.org/topic/strategic_approach/tags/gender/2088312.

International Fund for Agricultural Development (IFAD). 2014. Rural Youth. Evaluation Synthesis. Independent Office of Evaluation of IFAD. Rome: IFAD.

International Fund for Agricultural Development (IFAD). 2015. IFAD's Engagement with Indigenous Peoples. Evaluation Synthesis. Independent Office of Evaluation of IFAD. Rome: IFAD.

International Fund for Agricultural Development (IFAD). 2016a. FAO's and IFAD's Engagement in Pastoral Development. Joint Evaluation Synthesis. FAO's Evaluation Office and Independent Office of Evaluation of IFAD. Rome: IFAD.

International Fund for Agricultural Development (IFAD). 2016b. IFAD Strategic Framework 2016–2025. Rome: IFAD.

International Fund for Agricultural Development (IFAD). 2017. What Works for Gender Equality and Women's Empowerment – a Review of Practices and Results. Independent Office of Evaluation of IFAD. Rome: IFAD.

5 Evaluations for Sustainable Development

The 17 SDG goals and 169 targets are integrated and indivisible and balance the three dimensions of sustainable development: economic, social and environmental. This chapter will focus on the environmental dimension of sustainable development and will illustrate highlights from evaluations undertaken by IOE related to natural resources management, environment conservation in China and water conservation and management.

A. Evaluation and Natural Resources Management

A key principle underlying the 2030 Agenda is an 'integrated approach' to sustainable development across three dimensions – economic, social and environmental – with the overall aim of eradicating poverty, protecting the planet and securing prosperity (Sustainable Development Knowledge Platform website, n.d.).

IFAD's target group are the rural poor, many of whom live in fragile environments and depend critically on the natural resource base for their livelihoods and well-being. Addressing environmental degradation and ensuring environmental sustainability are therefore inextricably linked to IFAD's mandate to reduce rural poverty through investments in agriculture and rural development, positioning IFAD well to promote integrated approaches across multiple sectors.

It is in this context that in June 2016 IOE published an evaluation synthesis that analyses the results of IFAD's support to environment and natural resources management (ENRM) through an examination of evaluations conducted between 2010 and 2015.[1]

The past five years have seen an expansion of IFAD's attention to environmental issues, and significant steps at the corporate level mirror the evolution of IFAD's commitment to ENRM issues. The Environment and Climate Division was established, the environmental and social safeguards have been upgraded and the Adaptation for Smallholder Agriculture Programme has been launched. IFAD has combined a growing focus on 'avoiding harm' by assessing and managing environmental and social impacts with targeting its investments at "doing good" in the ENRM domain. In doing so, it has built on years of experience in community-based natural resources management.

Although data on ENRM content in loans are incomplete and probably understate the actual amount, they suggest some challenges in integrating environmental stewardship effectively into country programmes. The evidence from the analysis is that alignment with ENRM policies in IFAD country strategies is mixed during the period covered. A small number of COSOPs show a clear progression to a stronger focus on ENRM; others reveal a shift in the direction to other priority strategic areas, such as value chain investments, without necessarily paying attention to ENRM.

Taking a broader perspective, IFAD has clearly pursued the goal of improving the incomes and livelihoods of the rural poor through traditional natural resources management activities as well as more innovative projects that seek to bring about 'sustainable intensification'. These projects involve a more complex integrated approach, and are perhaps harder to track in terms of fund allocation and performance targets. Also, in contrast to the global environmental issues targeted by the Global Environment Facility and climate change targeted by the Adaptation for Smallholder Agriculture Programme, sustainable intensification lacks the impetus of a dedicated supplementary funding mechanism.

In order for IFAD to truly implement the goal of sustainable intensification of agricultural production, it needs to generate substantial incentives for farmers. Where demand for ENRM support from countries is limited, IFAD will also need to strengthen its efforts to foster greater integration of ENRM at the country level – clearly here the most feasible entry point is the COSOP – and there is a need to increase its country partners' understanding of how ENRM interventions contribute to poverty reduction. Equally, IFAD needs to improve its own data management of ENRM activities from tracking investments to measuring, monitoring and indeed evaluating ENRM performance.

B. Evaluation and Environment Conservation in China

In 2016, IOE carried out a project performance assessment of the Environment Conservation and Poverty-Reduction Programme in Ningxia and Shanxi, China.[2] The programme was implemented in one of the most remote and poorest areas in China – the Loess region, where serious environmental degradation in the country is occurring. The programme targeted 310,000 rural households, which included a significant share of Hui ethnic minority people in three programme counties in Ningxia.

The programme used a multi-sectoral approach to address the main causes of poverty within a fragile environment. Programme activities were implemented in the context of wider government efforts to reduce poverty in the region. The scale of the concerted efforts enabled a far-reaching transformation of the rural landscape, with significant improvements in basic education and health services, and consolidation of the natural resource base. Value was added through the consistent efforts to target programme benefits to the poorer households, in particular women. The extensive training that the programme provided was well received and met the existing demand.

The programme's benefits have been sustainable since completion in 2012, and they can be expected to be sustained for the foreseeable future. First, the government's commitment to poverty reduction and environmental conservation has been very strong, and President Xi Jinping has elevated the government's commitment to poverty reduction to an unprecedented high level. Second, the programme was implemented by government agencies and other organizations (including the All China Women's Federation and Rural Credit Cooperatives), which will almost certainly remain in place for many years to come. Third, most of the physical works which have supported improved agricultural productivity and human development outcomes have been reasonably well maintained, and the associated technology improvements have been widely adopted and can be expected to be retained until even better technologies eventually become available.

C. Evaluation and Water Conservation and Management

In 2014, IOE conducted an evaluation synthesis on water conservation and management.[3] The main objective of this synthesis was to capture how IFAD has responded to the emerging issues of rural water security and governance, whether IFAD's investments in water have met their intended objectives and are sustainable, and if it is possible to further enhance the effectiveness and sustainability of IFAD's investments in this sector. The synthesis reviewed not only the technical, environmental and financial aspects of investments made by IFAD, but also the social and institutional aspects where IFAD introduced the most interesting innovations. IFAD's policy work at national, regional and global levels on water-related issues was also reviewed.

In order to promote more sustainable and equitable water management practices, IFAD has joined forces with a global community of practice that encourages multiple water-use systems. These systems work to secure synergies in water use for different purposes, from different sources, by different people, at different times throughout the year. Land and water management interventions especially involving common property resources are most at risk of decline in the post-project period.

Overall, IFAD's engagement in the water sector has improved, starting from its country strategies, as a result of enhanced synergy between different project components and a greater alignment of the different instruments that IFAD deploys to achieve its strategic objectives. The scenario emerging on the water front presents a set of issues, challenges and opportunities such as: (i) water is both a constraint to development and an opportunity for innovation; (ii) water productivity is a game changer, critical to enhancing development effectiveness; and (iii) rainfed farming, undertaken by the bulk of poor smallholder farmers, is now key to increasing food production and agricultural productivity. This is where IFAD, in partnership with local governments and other development agencies, can take the lead in developing a strategy that can bring about a 'brown revolution' in rainfed agriculture akin to the 'green revolution' of irrigated agriculture.

With IFAD's comparative advantage in smallholder agriculture, and the need to increase food production in a sustainable manner within the context of increasing water scarcity and climate variability, IFAD's engagement in the water sector can only be expected to deepen in the years ahead.

Notes

1 International Fund for Agricultural Development (IFAD) (2016a).
2 International Fund for Agricultural Development (IFAD) (2016b).
3 International Fund for Agricultural Development (IFAD) (2014).

References

International Fund for Agricultural Development (IFAD). 2014. Water Conservation and Management. Evaluation Synthesis. Independent Office of Evaluation of IFAD. Rome: IFAD.

International Fund for Agricultural Development (IFAD). 2016a. Environment and Natural Resource Management. Evaluation Synthesis. Independent Office of Evaluation of IFAD. Rome: IFAD.

International Fund for Agricultural Development (IFAD). 2016b. Environment Conservation and Poverty-Reduction Programme in Ningxia and Shanxi, China. Project Performance Assessment. Independent Office of Evaluation of IFAD. Rome: IFAD.

Sustainable Development Knowledge Platform website: www.sustainabledevelopment.un.org/post2015/transformingourworld.

6 Learning and Knowledge Management

Decades of experience have shown that evaluations, however technically sound, do not automatically lead to changes in the design or implementation of programmes or strategies (Patton, 2008): design and implementation decisions are the responsibility of the management of the organizations and not the evaluators. However, there are institutional factors and conditions that can speed up or hinder the use of evaluations. Standards and instruments exist in IFAD to establish a route of utilization of evaluation results and provide Management and the Executive Board with the opportunity to monitor follow-up on recommendations. These instruments were introduced in 1999 for the first time and later refined with the introduction of the Evaluation Policy (2003) and its revision (2011).

A. Focus Groups to Facilitate Learning and Monitoring

From the beginning of an evaluation, IOE identifies a user focus group with which it shares and discusses a concept paper that outlines the scope, criteria, main questions, process and expected timeline of the evaluation. In the initial phases, this group helps to identify the priority issues to be addressed by the evaluation. During the main evaluation activities, members of the user focus group are consulted and the results and preliminary reports are shared with them. (See Figure 6.1)

B. President's Report on the Implementation Status of Evaluation Recommendations and Management Actions (PRISMA)

The full usefulness of an evaluation hinges on its potential to inform and improve future activities. Dissemination, learning and follow-up are crucial to the process. To this end, recommendations need to be presented in a form that allows different decision-makers to clearly identify their responsibilities, and track follow-up actions in IFAD's system. This process informs the PRISMA.

As required by the IFAD Evaluation Policy, each PRISMA contains an account of the follow-up actions taken by Management and the concerned

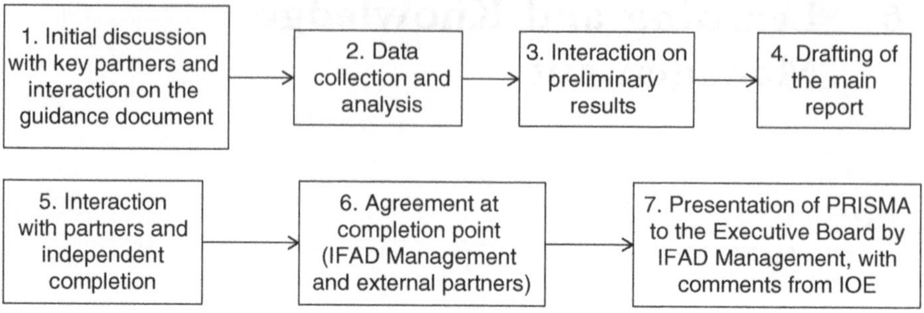

Figure 6.1 Outline of key interactions with partners in an evaluation process.

Source: Felloni, et.al.

government, where applicable, on the recommendations made by independent evaluations. This is an important instrument to promote learning and improvement and is presented each year to the Evaluation Committee and Executive Board, together with IOE's comments. It includes actions taken in response to recommendations made in the ARRI, CLEs, CSPEs, PPEs and evaluation synthesis reports.

In the ten years from 2006 to 2016, IFAD Management reported that it had received more than 1,900 recommendations from IOE stemming from its evaluations. In September 2016, for example, when Management presented the 13th edition of the PRISMA, it reviewed follow-up actions on 25 evaluations, 12 of which were undergoing continued, or 'historical' follow-up and review, and 13 of which were new evaluations finalized in 2014 and 2015. Some cases are profiled below.

The PRISMA covered four CLEs, 12 country-level evaluations and nine project-level evaluations. The CLEs dealt with: fragile states and situations; replenishments; supervision (second-round review); and efficiency (third-round review). It stated that Management's uptake of IOE recommendations stood at 94 per cent, confirming the upward trend in performance observed in recent editions of the PRISMA.

A disaggregated look at these results revealed a trend towards a greater number of corporate-level recommendations. As these required recurrent or longer-term actions, there was an increase in the percentage of recommendations which were ongoing. Consequently, there was a corresponding decline in the percentage of recommendations that were fully followed up at the report's issuance.

The PRISMA is the final step in a formal management response system at IFAD. The system was formally introduced in 1999, when the evaluation division, then known as the OE, launched the NEP. The system was based on the ACP prepared for country portfolio evaluations (now CSPEs).

The New Evaluation Process emphasized revitalizing the learning aspects from the various evaluations, in order to increase the effectiveness of IFAD's policies and programmes. It recognized that the users of evaluation recommendations needed to have a much greater level of involvement and participation in both the evaluation and response processes than had been the case previously.

The IFAD Evaluation Policy clearly indicates that IFAD Management and partners are responsible for implementing recommendations from evaluations, and for reporting on their implementation status to the Executive Board.

From Agreement at Completion Point to PRISMA

As per the IFAD Evaluation Policy and the Evaluation Manual, an ACP is prepared for CSPEs undertaken by IOE. The ACP is the joint response of IFAD Management and the concerned government, and is designed to address the recommendations contained in the final evaluation report. The responsibility for the timely completion of the ACP rests ultimately with IFAD Management and the concerned government. Working closely with the concerned government, PMD is responsible for drafting the ACP.

Once the ACP has been prepared, IFAD Management sends the document back to IOE, which then transmits the draft ACP to the government (copied to PMD) for its review and comments, or confirmation of the ACP. The ACP includes a section for comments in the final document, especially in the event of disagreement with any of the findings and/or recommendations contained in the evaluation.

The ACP is agreed upon between IFAD Management and the partner government, and the signed, final ACP should be ready within three months from the date of the evaluation learning workshop organized by IOE. The annual follow-up, provided through the PRISMA, is the responsibility of PMD. IOE comments on the analysis and the content of each PRISMA report.

Nowadays, the PRISMA includes follow-up actions taken to recommendations made in the ARRI, CLEs, CSPEs, PPEs and evaluation synthesis reports. The PRISMA also includes an account of how IOE comments on the Report on IFAD's Development Effectiveness have been treated by Management. For the ARRI, this includes recommendations agreed upon with the Board. For CSPEs, these are extracted from ACPs finalized at the end of the evaluation. For CLEs and evaluation synthesis reports, these are outlined in Management's responses or action plans submitted to and agreed by the Executive Board following evaluations. As far as PPEs are concerned, the PRISMA only includes the recommendations addressed to IFAD Management.

In terms of process, after the evaluations are selected, recommendations are extracted, listed and classified by selected themes for follow-up. The list is prepared by PMD and reviewed by IOE. The classification criteria used include level (e.g. country, project), nature (e.g. operational, strategic, policy) and theme.

The PRISMA report and IOE's comments on it, which are both reviewed by the Evaluation Committee and the Board (International Fund for Agricultural Development, 2013, 2014, 2015, 2016), were cited as an evaluation best practice in a study by the Swedish Agency for Development Evaluation in its report, 'IFAD's Management Response System - The Agreement at Completion Point Process' (Bandstein and Hedblom, 2008).

PRISMA Closes the Learning Loop

By Caroline Heider, former IOE Deputy Director (from 2005 to 2006)

When I arrived at IFAD in 2005, one of my many tasks was to work with my counterpart in PMD, Shyam Khadka, on a report that summarized what had been done in response to recommendations of evaluations. My task was two-fold: find a better name, which bemused me; and find a way to make the report more useful to programme management, which was the basis for a strong collaborative effort between Shyam and me. The first task was easily accomplished and the name PRISMA was born. The second task took much greater effort, in particular on the part of Shyam and his colleague Theresa Rice.

The challenge consisted in giving greater structure and sense to the cumulative recommendations IOE had issued. Each derived from the various evaluations that had been completed over the year. But the list of recommendations was a rather diverse set of things, ranging from rather small operational matters to big strategic shifts. In this maze of recommendations, it was hard to see whether recommendations pointed to organization-wide issues rather than isolated problems.

Therefore, our first agreement was to categorize the recommendations and understand better what they were signalling collectively. This allowed the recommendations and responses to be summarized in different ways, shifting from simply listing them to highlighting whether the majority of recommendations involved smaller adjustments or larger systemic changes. In my view, this was the greatest value-added that we generated in those early years of PRISMA; something Shyam and his colleagues continued to build on.

In hindsight, we at IOE could have made better use of these insights to think through whether we played as strategic a role as we could with our evaluation work.

One challenge, however, that remained during the two years Shyam and I collaborated was the quality and veracity of the responses. As we reviewed responses together we could tell when someone effectively engaged with a set of recommendations and had meaningful responses. Likewise, it was easy to detect – but not prove – when that was not so. A system that relies on reports that can be validated only through desk-based reviews rather than on-site visits will always face these limitations. For those recommendations that should manifest changes in partner countries, it might be possible to close that information gap by tapping into continuously expanding data sources to corroborate reported change.

C. Knowledge Management and the Philippines Country Strategy and Programme Evaluation

In 2016, IOE conducted a CSPE in the Philippines and identified knowledge management as a central feature of IFAD's support, describing the country strategy as a knowledge-driven partnership. IOE pointed to the experience in the Philippines as one which could be used to inform the design of initiatives in other settings. Still, evaluators noted, knowledge-sharing initiatives did not always have the desired impact on policymakers (International Fund for Agricultural Development, 2017).

The Philippines CSPE is an example of how IOE evaluations give prominence to knowledge management. IFAD's Knowledge Management Strategy identifies a limited number of knowledge themes, derived from the IFAD Strategic Framework 2007–2010. Its approach: builds incrementally on IFAD's existing assets, processes and partnerships; identifies the specific instruments needed to improve learning and knowledge-sharing at the country programme level; identifies the cultural and behavioral changes needed for implementation and the incentives and training that must be put in place to bring these changes about; and seeks to ensure cost-effectiveness by harnessing resources and efforts and integrating them into a coherent and time-bound results framework.

The strategy has four strategic components: strengthening knowledge-sharing and learning processes; equipping IFAD with a more supportive knowledge-sharing and learning infrastructure; fostering partnerships for broader knowledge-sharing and learning; and promoting a supportive knowledge-sharing and learning culture.

Context. In 2016, the Philippines had one of the fastest-growing economies in Southeast Asia, but poverty among its 55 million rural inhabitants was well over twice the rate faced by its 45 million urban residents. For the Philippines, knowledge management received prominent attention in IFAD's 2009 country strategy, as an element which held the potential to stimulate innovation and bridge the gap between grants and loan projects.

Findings. In the evaluation, IOE found that knowledge management was well set out as an integrated part of the country programme. It was also appropriately resourced and inclusive. There were clear objectives, and structured mechanisms, which IFAD used effectively. Annual country programme reviews and 'Knowledge and Learning Markets' proved popular with implementers as a means of sharing experience, and enabled cross-fertilization of ideas.

Knowledge management features in all country strategies, but in the Philippines a number of supportive and related factors worked together to make this a core feature. Firstly, the loans programme had several innovative elements, for which policy dialogue was identified to be important; secondly, the dialogue was to be promoted through a series of participatory processes; thirdly, the period covered by this review coincided with a shift to direct supervision and the establishment of an in-country office, with the appointment of a country programme management facilitator/knowledge management officer (a title that was later simplified to country programme officer).

With a country programme officer in place and a clear mandate, knowledge management developed three distinct but supportive strands: annual country portfolio reviews by staff from loan and grant projects, together with representatives of partner government departments and agencies; annual two-day Knowledge and Learning Markets (stimulated at first by a regional programme, Knowledge Networking for Rural Development in the Asia/Pacific Region) that bring together non-governmental organizations, the private sector, research institutions, government, project staff and the general public and are hosted by a different one of these groups each year; and the IFAD Philippines Gender Network of project gender focal points, civil society organizations and implementing agencies.

Results. The annual country portfolio meetings ensured a regular and rigorous review of the portfolio, comparing performance across projects and making good use of analysis by independent national consultants. The knowledge management activities provided a platform for wider policy discussion and are credited with cross-fertilization of ideas across grants and loan projects.

Specifically, discussions at the meetings contributed to the redesign of a credit programme in the Cordillera into the Livelihood Assistance Fund, patterned after the Poverty Alleviation Fund of Northern Mindanao, and gave rise to the decision to fund a study to reform cost-sharing arrangements between national and local government that were holding back infrastructure development. A model mechanism for supervision at community level that started as Community-based Operation & Maintenance Monitoring and Evaluation Teams in Northern Mindanao was adapted as Barangay Planning, Monitoring and Evaluation Teams in the Cordillera Highlands project.

The joint forum for grants and loan projects enabled linkages to be formed over and above expectations, and with a number of innovations, including: introducing Farmer Business Schools, using experience from the FoodSTART project with the International Potato Centre (known by its Spanish acronym CIP); cataloguing and developing the value chain for heirloom rice varieties in the Cordillera region by the International Rice Research Institute project on rice in unfavourable environments; and introducing payments for environmental services by the World Agroforestry Centre.

Five of the nine Knowledge and Learning Markets studied were hosted by non-governmental organizations, with themes that ranged from community initiatives, to gender and youth, to resilient family farming. This demonstrated a level of engagement that was broader than IFAD's portfolio of projects, and created a community of interest around IFAD's support.

Challenges. A central question in international development is how knowledge can best be generated, mobilized, made available, applied and adapted to improve the human condition. The experience in the Philippines highlights positive lessons and some challenges to make knowledge management more effective. Having in-country staff whose terms of reference clearly included knowledge management and a clear direction was important.

Annual reviews were always strongly supported by IFAD headquarters and included representatives from government departments and agencies. Knowledge events provided a platform for civil society organizations alongside project and government entities. This built on the strong tradition of 'people power' in the Philippines and gave rise to some notable results, including a set of eleven policy briefs stimulated by the International Year of Family Farming.

Not everything lived up to the expectations of the 2009 country strategy. Lessons from implementation had clear policy implications, but they largely reflected tools and techniques – evidence about activities rather than development results and higher-level strategic issues.

Project arrangements for monitoring and evaluation failed to deliver messages about poverty reduction and implementation effectiveness. The lessons from the projects provide potential leverage for IFAD to engage with the government on the design and implementation of relevant rural and agricultural development initiatives. But there was no obvious link between discussions in these knowledge forums and interaction over sectoral policy issues.

Few senior government officials participated in the knowledge management events and neither were there participants from partner development organizations. The challenge going forward is to find a way to communicate findings and guidance from contacts at project level, into concepts that resonate with policymakers.

References

Bandstein, S. and Hedblom, E. 2008. IFAD's Management Response System. Karlstad: Swedish Agency for Development Evaluation.

International Fund for Agricultural Development. 2013. President's Report on the Implementation Status of Evaluation Recommendations and Management Actions (PRISMA). Volume I and Volume II. EB 2013/109/R.13. Rome: IFAD.

International Fund for Agricultural Development. 2014. President's Report on the Implementation Status of Evaluation Recommendations and Management Actions (PRISMA). Volume I and Volume II. EB 2014/112/R.5. Rome: IFAD.

International Fund for Agricultural Development. 2015. President's Report on the Implementation Status of Evaluation Recommendations and Management Actions (PRISMA). Volume I and Volume II. EB 2015/115/R.5. Rome: IFAD.

International Fund for Agricultural Development. 2016. President's Report on the Implementation Status of Evaluation Recommendations and Management Actions (PRISMA). Volume I and Volume II. EB 2016/118/R.10. Rome: IFAD.

International Fund for Agricultural Development. 2017. Republic of the Philippines Country Strategy and Programme Evaluation. Independent Office of Evaluation. Rome: IFAD.

Patton, M.Q. 2008. *Utilization-Focused Evaluation*, 4th edition. Thousand Oaks, CA: Sage Publications.

7 Partnerships in Evaluation

SDG 17, which reads 'Strengthen the means of implementation and revitalize the Global Partnership for Sustainable Development', recognizes multi-stakeholder partnerships as important vehicles for mobilizing and sharing knowledge, expertise, technologies and financial resources to support the achievement of the SDGs in all countries. In this context, partnership-building in evaluation is critical to enhance the poverty reduction impact and effectiveness of IFAD-supported initiatives. To this end, IOE has been active in creating and strengthening partnerships with the ECG of multilateral development banks, the other Rome-based agencies, the UNEG, evaluation associations (global and regional), countries such as Switzerland and other key evaluation partners.

A. Evaluation Cooperation Group

As previously mentioned, ECG promotes a more harmonized approach to evaluation methodology among its members, which are multilateral development financial institutions. IFAD has been a member of the ECG since 2010, and is the chair of ECG for 2017, hosting the ECG spring and fall meetings.

B. Rome-Based Agencies Collaboration

In April 2013, the evaluation offices of IFAD and three other Rome-based agencies, the CGIAR (formerly known as Consultative Group on International Agricultural Research), FAO and WFP, issued, for the first time, a joint statement calling for closer collaboration on evaluation among their agencies. The following are examples of Rome-based agencies' collaboration in evaluation:

- Evaluation synthesis on pastoral development, undertaken jointly by FAO and IFAD evaluation offices[1]
- International conference on the evaluability of SDG2, organized jointly by CGIAR, FAO, IFAD AND WFP[2]

C. United Nations Evaluation Group

IOE is a founding member of the UNEG, an inter-agency professional network that brings together the evaluation units of the United Nations system and affiliated organizations. Its mission is to promote the independence, credibility and usefulness of the evaluation function and evaluation across the United Nations system, to advocate for the importance of evaluation for learning, decision-making and accountability, and to support the evaluation community in the United Nations system and beyond. As an example of its strong relation with UNEG, IOE hosted UNEG's extraordinary Annual Meeting at IFAD headquarters in September 2013. The purpose of the meeting was to finalize UNEG's strategy for the coming years.

D. Evaluation and Global or Regional Associations

IOE is a member of and/or collaborates with various evaluation and regional associations that promote learning and knowledge-sharing. These institutions organize events that bring together evaluators and professionals from diverse backgrounds and disciplines. IOE periodically leads sessions or delivers presentations on themes such as supporting learning and organizational effectiveness – the communication function of IOE; contributing to rural poverty reduction through accountability and learning; and evaluation architecture to support learning and accountability. Brief information about some of these associations follows.

- African Evaluation Association.[3] This Association was founded in 1999, in response to Africa's growing appeal for advocacy, information-sharing and advanced capacity-building in evaluation. The organization's chief focus is to counter limited evaluation opportunities by building strategic bridges for African evaluators to connect, network and share experiences.
- American Evaluation Association.[4] This is a professional association of evaluators devoted to the application and exploration of programme evaluation, personnel evaluation, technology and many other forms of evaluation.
- Australasian Evaluation Society.[5] This society works to improve the theory, practice and use of evaluation in Australasia for people involved in evaluation including evaluation practitioners, managers, teachers and students of evaluation, and other interested individuals.
- European Evaluation Society.[6] This society's activities aim to support improved enabling environments for evaluation, stronger communities of practice, relevant evaluation research and enhanced evaluation methods. It seeks to advance evaluation knowledge and to encourage adoption of good practices by fostering evaluation excellence, independence and partnerships.
- International Development Evaluation Association.[7] This association was inaugurated in September 2002 to meet the need for a global professional association for internationally active development evaluators. Over the

years, much has changed in the global evaluation community. Many new national and regional associations have been created. Global partnerships and communities of practice have been formed, allowing joint efforts between both evaluation professional associations and organizations.

- Latin America and the Caribbean Network for Monitoring, Evaluation and Systematization.[8] This network is oriented toward strengthening the practice and culture of M&E in Latin American and the Caribbean countries. Its mission is to influence and improve projects, programmes and policies, as well as contribute to strengthening civil society participation and transparency.

E. Evaluation Partnership with Switzerland

A first Swiss Agency for Development Cooperation–IFAD agreement, called 'Partnership on development effectiveness through evaluation', was signed in May 2001. The partnership was implemented over a three-year period, from 2001 to 2004, and included original grant financing of CHF1.5 million (US$1.6 million) to be administered by IFAD and devoted exclusively to financing IOE evaluation activities. The partnership was extended to a second phase in 2004 and a third phase in 2009, for an additional financing of CHF3 million (US$3.2 million). A new (fourth) phase of the cooperation was signed in June 2013, for a duration of three years with an additional contribution of CHF950,000 (US$1 million). Although the formulation of the partnership objectives may have changed in the various phases, the core priorities were to: invest in innovation to test new methodologies, models and approaches to evaluation, which could eventually be mainstreamed through the regular administrative budget; support the development of IFAD's self-evaluation capabilities through strengthening project-level M&E systems, including the further harmonization of self-evaluation and independent evaluation methodologies; and promote learning and strengthening knowledge exchange with the Swiss Agency, IFAD and others on lessons learned and insights on key thematic issues emerging from evaluations of agriculture and rural development projects and programmes (IFAD and Swiss Agency for Development and Cooperation, 2014).

Key evaluations conducted by IOE and financed by the Swiss Agency are the United Republic of Tanzania CPE and the first ARRI (2003); the CLE on IFAD's Direct Supervision Pilot Programme and the Independent External Evaluation of IFAD (2005); the CLE on the Field Presence Pilot Programme (2007); the Joint Evaluation with AfDB on Agriculture and Rural Development in Africa (2009); the CLEs on IFAD's Capacity to Promote Innovation and Scaling Up and on Gender (2010); the CLE on IFAD's Institutional Efficiency and Efficiency of IFAD-funded Operations (2013); and the CLE on IFAD Replenishments (2014).

F. Cooperation for Evaluation Capacity Development

- People's Republic of China. On 23 September 2013, the Government of China (Ministry of Finance) and IOE signed a Statement of Intent to forge a partnership for cooperation of evaluation capacity development. The objective of establishing this partnership is to contribute to development of evaluation capacities for agriculture and rural poverty alleviation interventions in China. This initiative is in line with IOE's strategic objectives and is based on the growing need to strengthen national evaluation capacity in the agriculture and rural sectors in recipient countries.

- Shanghai International Program for Development Evaluation Training.[9] This programme is committed to promoting development evaluation capacity-building in China and other Asian developing countries through a range of activities, such as training workshops, research and network-building. IOE attends and delivers presentations at the biannual SHIPDET in China, as part of the IOE-supported evaluation capacity development programme.

G. Wilton Park

Wilton Park is an international forum for strategic discussion that focuses on issues of international security, prosperity and justice. Wilton Park organizes over 60 events a year in the United Kingdom and overseas, bringing together leading representatives from the worlds of politics, diplomacy, academia, business, civil society, the military and the media. Every year, IOE actively participates in selected Wilton Park events.[10]

Notes

1 www.ifad.org/evaluation/reports/evaluation_synthesis/tags/livestock/y2016/9963916
2 www.ifad.org/evaluation/event/tags/y2015/7979619
3 www.afrea.org/
4 www.eval.org/
5 www.aes.asn.au/about-us.html
6 www.europeanevaluation.org/
7 www.ideas-global.org/
8 www.noticiasrelac.ning.com/
9 www.afdc.org.cn/SAG_html.aspx?h=5&l=english&Type=SHIPDET
10 www.wiltonpark.org.uk/about-us/

Reference

IFAD and Swiss Agency for Development and Cooperation. 2014. *Independent Office of Evaluation of IFAD and Swiss Agency for Development and Cooperation: A Partnership for Better Results*. Rome: IFAD.

8 The Way Forward

International organizations, governments and communities face new challenges as they seek to improve social and economic conditions, but they also have new opportunities to make a positive difference. IFAD's mandate to contribute to sustainable and inclusive rural transformation is more relevant than ever, and its capacity to measure and build on its impact, learning from experience through evaluation, will continue to play a crucial role in enhancing the quality of its interventions geared towards achieving its mandate.

A. Agenda 2030 and the Sustainable Development Goals

Context

Many rural farmers face significant constraints in accessing resources and technology. They run up against barriers in access to transport, information and financing, which limits their participation in input and product markets. A lack of access to modern farming technologies, and consequently lower crop yields and limited diets, increases the risk of hunger and malnourishment.

In September 2015, United Nations Member States formalized a vision for a 'plan of action for people, planet and prosperity',[1] by adopting Agenda 2030, a global commitment to realize 17 SDGs. These goals are hinged on the achievement of 169 targets, which have indicators and means of implementation, and a pledge to 'leave no one behind' in moving towards a more equitable and sustainable future.

Unlike the Millennium Development Goals (MDGs), which guided development and poverty reduction efforts through 2015, Agenda 2030 is universal. Rather than focusing only on developing countries, it applies to states and territories at all levels of development. It is also far more ambitious than the MDGs, in that it aims to eradicate poverty and hunger and to put all economies and societies on a sustainable path.

The SDGs cut across social, environmental and economic issues, as well as governance and means of implementation. Many of these goals fall squarely within the domain of IFAD's work to eradicate rural poverty and food insecurity and to make investments to raise smallholder productivity and incomes, but progress on any goal requires coordinated action on others.

IFAD and the Sustainable Development Goals[2]

The SDGs are interconnected and cross-cutting. No SDG can be fully realized without support to the others.

IFAD's mandate gives it a central role in contributing to the achievement of the following:

- **SDG 1** - No poverty: End poverty in all its forms everywhere.
- **SDG 2** - Zero hunger: End hunger, achieve food security and improved nutrition and promote sustainable agriculture.
- **SDG 10** - Reduced inequalities: Reduce inequalities within and among countries.

By supporting the empowerment of rural women, IFAD also brings a major contribution to:

- **SDG 5** - Gender equality: Achieve gender equality and empower all women and girls.

By fostering inclusive, diversified and productive rural economies, IFAD contributes to:

- **SDG 8** - Decent work and economic growth: Promote sustained, inclusive and sustainable economic growth, full and productive employment and decent work for all.
- **SDG 9** - Industry, innovation and infrastructure: Build resilient infrastructure, promote inclusive and sustainable industrialization, and foster innovation.
- **SDG 11** - Sustainable cities and communities: Make cities and human settlements inclusive, safe, resilient and sustainable.

By investing in sustainable agriculture and smallholder adaptation capacity to climate change, IFAD supports:

- **SDG 6** - Clean water and sanitation: Ensure availability and sustainable management of water and sanitation for all.
- **SDG 12** - Responsible consumption and production: Ensure sustainable consumption and production patterns.
- **SDG 13** - Climate action: Take urgent action to combat climate change and its impacts.
- **SDG 14** - Life below water: Conserve and sustainably use the oceans, seas and marine resources for sustainable development.
- **SDG 15** - Life on land: Protect, restore and promote sustainable use of terrestrial ecosystems, sustainably manage forests, combat desertification, and halt and reverse land degradation and halt biodiversity loss.

By strengthening local institutions and natural resources governance, IFAD supports:

- **SDG 16** - Peace, justice and strong institutions: Promote peaceful and inclusive societies for sustainable development, provide access to justice for all, and build effective, accountable and inclusive institutions at all levels.

B. Evaluation and the Sustainable Development Goals

Some insights into the process of evaluating work on the SDGs were gained soon after Agenda 2030 was adopted. In November 2015, IFAD hosted a technical seminar, *Enhancing the evaluability of Sustainable Development Goal 2: End hunger, achieve food security and improved nutrition, and promote sustainable agriculture,*[3] which was jointly organized by the evaluation offices of the Rome-based United Nations agencies: CGIAR, FAO, IFAD and WFP.

The objective of the seminar was to contribute to a shared understanding of how SDG 2 could be evaluated and to identify actions needed to enable evaluations of SDG 2 throughout the United Nations system, other international organizations, or member countries themselves. The process offered takeaways of relevance to the challenges facing the overall evaluation process (International Fund for Agricultural Development, 2015a, 2015b).

More than 160 people attended, representing national governments, 35 countries, academia, think tanks, the private sector and United Nations organizations, while about 1,000 people followed the event online.

The seminar provided an opportunity to: share lessons learned from previous monitoring and evaluation of the MDGs, and other partnership initiatives of similar scale; jointly review key challenges for evaluation in relation to the post-2015 development agenda in general and SDG 2 in particular; and identify concrete steps for the Rome-based agencies to take in their approach to evaluating progress made with respect to SDG 2.

Thematic discussions included:

- The relevance of 'new metrics' for the evaluation of SDG 2 – data revolution and innovative approaches for assessing human well-being (e.g. food availability, nutrition and food security and their implications in humanitarian/development contexts).
- Partnerships and development actors – dealing with the increasing complexity of development processes and implications for evaluation (e.g. complex partnerships, various actors within countries).
- National monitoring and evaluation systems and data availability – building on the progress made and addressing existing capacity gaps.
- Demand for and use of evidence from evaluation – understanding the political economy of evidence, or why certain interventions or decisions may be

preferred by political leaders to others, and developing a joint evaluation agenda for SDG 2.

Among the challenges noted was the need for Rome-based agencies to be flexible in their thinking as they encounter new and more complex partnerships, as they sift through a vast list of indicators for the SDGs, and as they attempt to reconcile varying definitions of key concepts such as food security, sustainable agriculture and malnutrition.

The global data architecture reveals uneven availability of data among countries. This is sobering considering that what we cannot measure also matters. Concretely, in IFAD's work, this translates into lack of systematic data on food storage, food losses and waste. There is lack of data on the nutritional status of children, adolescents and pregnant women. Agricultural statistics suffer from limited funding and lack of consistency. For example, it is challenging to assess the percentage of agricultural area under sustainable agricultural practices, the percentage of agricultural households using irrigation systems compared to all agricultural households, or the percentage of agricultural households using eco-friendly fertilizers compared to all agricultural households using fertilizers. Similar challenges apply to a variety of the SDGs.

C. The Opportunities and Challenges of New Technologies

The Advent of Information and Communication Technologies

The evolution of the international development landscape will require improved methods, new technologies and speedier processes, from more impact-oriented evaluation planning to quicker delivery of feedback and response (e.g. during the project cycle, rather than at the close of a project). It will also require greater use of the information, knowledge and recommendations gained from evaluations. New technologies offer the potential to enhance the evaluation cycle, including planning and execution, feedback and management response, and the sharing of knowledge with partners.

Experience shows that evaluators face recurring challenges, especially in the field, due to lack of reliable M&E data, in addition to limited resources. ICTs used in development are providing new methods of gathering, analysing and disseminating data, changing the way in which evaluations are conducted.

Today, satellite signals, mobile telecommunications antennas, and TV and radio frequencies cover the globe. According to the International Telecommunication Union, more than 85 per cent of the world's population lives in areas covered by 2G mobile networks that allow the transfer of some data, and 70 per cent of the world's population is covered by 3G or better technologies, allowing fast access to the World Wide Web through mobile phones or other wireless networked devices.

Other technologies which are having an impact on agriculture and the evaluation of agricultural, rural and poverty reduction initiatives include remote-sensing technologies, digital survey applications and data analysis powered by machine learning and artificial intelligence. Evaluators now have at their disposal an impressive array of tools that can be deployed in almost any setting. ICTs show great potential in contributing to the quality of their work.

ICTs are critical to strengthening evidence-based policymaking, which relies on the evaluation of impacts, outcomes and shortcomings of development initiatives at all levels of activity. But they are not a magic wand to resolve all problems. Like any tool, they must be assessed for their relevance and availability, and the people who use them need to be informed. Evaluators, therefore, need to keep abreast of key developments in the field of ICTs, in order to stay on the cutting edge of innovation, and to continue to shape the future of development evaluation.

Evaluators must necessarily address a series of questions as they consider the new technologies. Can ICTs contribute to solving the daily challenges of development evaluators? Are evaluators using the most innovative tools and methodologies at their disposal? Can evaluators of development do better, and can more be done? How can the use of ICTs affect evaluation methodology and ethics? What is their potential impact on sampling bias, exclusion, data security and privacy?

One issue to be explored, for example, is the potential risk involved in making the practice of evaluation techno-centric, thus moving away from multi-dimensional approaches, which are vital when conducting evaluations across different contexts and cultures.

Knowledge-Sharing on ICTs

IOE organized an international conference on Information and Communication Technologies for Evaluation (ICT4Eval), which took place on 6 and 7 June 2017 at IFAD headquarters. The purpose was to discuss recent innovations in ICTs and demonstrable benefits to the intersecting fields of development evaluation and rural transformation; the latest innovative approaches to the use of ICTs in evaluation; and best practices that have emerged from the experiences of development organizations and private-sector actors around the world.

The event was organized around three main topics: ICTs applied to data collection; ICTs applied to data analysis; and ICTs applied to data dissemination. The programme included four panel sessions, 15 breakout sessions and 36 speakers. The conference gathered more than 200 experts from across the development field, including technical staff from UNEG and representatives from: the ECG; bilateral and multilateral development and humanitarian organizations; the private sector; academic institutions; non-governmental organizations; foundations; think tanks; and national-level counterparts from evaluation and policy institutions. They shared their knowledge and experience in using ICTs to improve the effectiveness of evaluation and to strengthen development impact (International Fund for Agricultural Development, 2017).

Parallel to the conference, a Tech Fair with 12 vendors and exhibitors was held on 7 June, which provided the opportunity for interaction and networking among development evaluators and service providers of ICT tools. The Tech Fair enabled participants to concretely anchor the discussions during the breakout sessions in a hands-on way, seeing what the latest tools look like and their implications.

Evaluations have historically depended on document reviews, observations and interviews during field visits. However, newer tools and sources for data collection and analysis have emerged in recent years and stem from three main elements: advances in the availability of remote sensing systems; widespread availability and use of wireless technology; and the possibility of integrating tools for machine learning and predictive modelling with other data sources. These advances are leading to an increasing level of automation and integration of data collection and analysis, thus making them faster, more accurate and less expensive.

During the ICT conference, five breakout sessions were dedicated to data collection topics and included simulated field visits in conflict environments, using geospatial tools for remote sensing, Earth observation to support evaluation, Collect Earth as an innovative and free land-monitoring tool, and different perspectives on the potential of mobile-based data collection tools. During the sessions, participants learned how ICTs can provide real-time data for remote M&E in restricted areas, maintaining integrity and quality of evidence. Extensive discussions took place on how remote sensing can complement existing methods of data collection and potentially open up newer avenues as well. The tools and capacities required to use remote sensing and earth observation were also discussed. Mobile-based data collection tools were found to be time-savers, but challenges relating to selection methods, training, infrastructure and acceptance need to be addressed.

Collecting large quantities of data is not an end in itself, but a way to facilitate informed decision-making. Using this as a bridge to the second theme of the conference – data analysis – a panel discussion took place on the role of big data. The panel discussed how big data can be used in a variety of ways and contexts and offers opportunities for real-time monitoring. At the same time there are privacy issues surrounding the use of big data and potential inequalities it may create in access. The need for bridge-building between data development centres and evaluation departments to learn from and appreciate each other's strengths is a key issue as we move forward.

Reflections. Before the conference was concluded, summarizing thoughts and reflections for the future were provided by Ms Caroline Heider, Director General and Senior Vice President, Independent Evaluation Group, World Bank Group and Mr Marco Segone, Director, Independent Evaluation Office, UN Women. It was suggested that evaluators should aim not to repeat past mistakes by continuing to dichotomize quantitative and qualitative data. Instead, they should increase the use of mixed methods, always aiming to seek out the right tool for the right question. Technology in itself is not the solution: humans are needed to teach the machine to learn, and humans are then needed to interpret the data once the data have been processed. To do this, however, humans need to be open to new forms of knowledge and change.

With regard to the concept of holistic evaluations, the vision should be to build more integrated data systems and to expand the ICT capacities of partners, empowering them to make much better sense of their own contextual data and development.

The topic of big data and the opportunities it offers for providing real-time evaluations was further explored. The recommendation was that social justice and human rights should always be put at the centre, including ownership and interpretation of data. Otherwise, there is a risk of increasing inequalities by not capturing those left behind or excluding stakeholders by simply extracting data.

Regarding data usage, ICTs bring many possibilities for monitoring migrant flows through mobile signals that can be used positively by humanitarian organizations, but also in a very different way by the parties that are in conflict. This risk of unintended and problematic uses need to be considered carefully.

ICTs are a train that has already left the station and will accelerate with or without the evaluators. Therefore, the evaluation community should neither resist nor embrace ICTs in evaluation, but should shape them so that they can influence not only how evaluators use ICTs but create a culture of ICT usage that can be shared and influence partners as well.

The overall conclusion by both panellists was that ICTs are not a panacea and that big data does not always mean better data. In the end, evaluators should familiarize themselves with the application of ICTs so that they are able to determine when to apply them, and to ask for external specialization when needed. Moreover, requests for expertise often result in increased partnerships with young evaluators, since they are the ones who were born into the new technology era.

Concluding remarks. Mr Oscar A. Garcia closed the conference by mirroring what Haishan Fu had said during the opening – behind every data point there is a human story. In the end, technology is only a tool to improve the effectiveness and efficiency of evaluations and ICTs are only as good as the evaluator who uses them.

On a practical note, 'evaluators are first evaluators and not technology wizards'. Although more resources and capacities should be geared towards mainstreaming technology into evaluation work, the key lies in tapping into complementary and shared capacities with partners. For IFAD, this means expanding collaboration with the Rome-based agencies, but also new collaborations with the private sector, non-governmental organizations, academia and others.

It is necessary to overcome 'organization inertia' and to learn, innovate and grow. Moving into the future, it will be vital to have an open mind and recognize that this is just the beginning of a long iterative journey about how to keep improving our evidence-based work.

D. The Private Sector

IFAD is moving decisively into engaging the private sector in the operations it funds. Private-sector entities play a central role in smallholder agriculture and rural development, offering opportunities for the creation of employment and wealth in rural areas. Their contribution in promoting access to markets, undertaking innovations, providing essential services – including technical assistance, training and rural finance – and supplying inputs has proven to be complementary and critical to the services provided by government agencies, and non-governmental and civil society organizations. In partnership with governments, they are increasingly active in infrastructure development and the delivery of public goods and services. Yet, with notable exceptions, private-sector interventions are not routinely subjected to systematic evaluative scrutiny. This new reality poses a number of challenges and requires significant adjustments to the way development evaluation is undertaken in terms of methodologies and processes. First of all, evaluation outfits need to adopt new, tailored methodologies and indicators for assessing the role and contribution of the private sector in the development efforts promoted by multilateral organizations. This means understanding what the private sector brings in and what methodologies and indicators can be used to evaluate and assess its contribution and participation.

E. Towards 2030

This chapter has looked at some of the changes which are occurring in the development arena and which, going forward, will require profound reflection by all evaluators. The adoption of the SDGs presents a common vision, and the SDGs provide guidance through targets and indicators. At the same time, they present new questions about the most effective ways to measure progress and increase the impact of the work undertaken by IFAD and its partners in the United Nations, in governments, in private-sector entities, and in communities around the globe. Finding the answers is an ongoing task.

In its unique role as both a specialized agency of the United Nations system and an IFI, IFAD has a clear vision of its role to facilitate both public and private investment, support national and global policy processes, generate and share knowledge, and develop partnerships through which marginalized groups find greater opportunities to benefit while playing a full and active role.

IFAD's main instruments for delivery are loan-funded projects and programmes, which it helps governments, smallholders and other stakeholders to develop and implement. The Fund also has a small grant-financing window. The scaling-up of IFAD's results and impact are a top priority.

In this context, knowledge management, partnerships and policy dialogue continue to be essential means for IFAD to achieve its goals. Through its partnerships and cofinancing arrangements, IFAD seeks to leverage its own resources, experience and knowledge, all of which are essential for scaled-up impact, whether in meetings with community members, government ministers, private-sector investors, or at international fora for strategic discussions like the events hosted by Wilton Park (as mentioned in Chapter 7 on partnerships).

Looking forward, IFAD will continue to focus on the areas it knows and on which it has built its reputation, while at the same time working in partnership with others to address development challenges that go beyond its area of specialization, or to leverage its experience and knowledge for greater development impact.

This agenda reinforces the role of evaluation in IFAD, to assess the Fund's development impact, to examine and assess what works, for whom, where, when and why, and to understand the pathways to change. Evaluation plays an important role in the way IFAD's business model, operational focus, corporate processes and accountability systems evolve. Evaluations that are put to use in strengthening the impact of IFAD's work ensure that the Fund is in the best possible position to fulfil its mandate and meet its corporate goals, especially in rapidly changing development contexts.

In line with the IFAD Evaluation Policy, IOE evaluations will continue to be used as critical instruments to promote accountability for results and learning for improved effectiveness. Results relative to targets in the RMF and other commitments agreed upon with Member States will be reported annually to the Executive Board and its Evaluation Committee in the Report on IFAD's Development Effectiveness[4] and the ARRI produced by IOE, as well as at the mid-term reviews of IFAD's replenishments.

The Strategic Framework, along with the RMF and commitments agreed upon with governing bodies, will be key elements of IFAD's performance planning and management system, consisting of: three-year medium-term plans to ensure that operations, workforce and finances are focused on fulfilling commitments and targets; a results-based budgeting system to promote optimal and economical use of internal resources; and a proactive internal results monitoring system to facilitate prompt remedial action by Management as performance issues arise.

Amid the new issues, new objectives, changing targets and indicators, IFAD will need to be able to adjust its programmes, policies and strategies, and the evaluation function will need to evolve as well, to facilitate a constant and fluid process of accountability and learning. New demands are continually being placed on IFAD's ability to understand rural transformation and to report on results in new areas, on its capacity to measure new dimensions of poverty, and on its data, evaluation tools, approaches and methodologies.

Effectiveness, relevance, credibility, rigour, flexibility and innovation in evaluation will continue to be essential ingredients in forward-looking development policies, programmes and projects that have been designed, implemented and evaluated to help transform the lives – and livelihoods – of the poor rural people of the world.

Notes

1 https://sustainabledevelopment.un.org/post2015/transformingourworld
2 www.ifad.org/topic/overview/tags/sdgs.
3 www.ifad.org/evaluation/event/tags/y2015/7979619.
4 The annual report on IFAD's Development Effectiveness (RIDE) presents the main features of IFAD's performance in three broad areas, namely: the relevance of IFAD's mandate and operations in the context of the changing framework of international development assistance; the development effectiveness of IFAD-financed operations in generating development results "on the ground" that support national and global efforts to reduce rural poverty and contribute to achieving the Millennium Development Goals, and the first MDG in particular; and the organizational effectiveness and efficiency of the Fund in delivering those results through improved internal performance management.

References

International Fund for Agricultural Development. IFAD and the Sustainable Development Goals website: www.ifad.org/topic/overview/tags/sdgs.

International Fund for Agricultural Development. 2015a. Enhancing the Evaluability of Sustainable Development Goal 2. Concept Note. Independent Office of Evaluation of IFAD. Rome: IFAD.

International Fund for Agricultural Development. 2015b. Enhancing the Evaluability of Sustainable Development Goal 2. Proceedings. Independent Office of Evaluation of IFAD. Rome: IFAD.

International Fund for Agricultural Development. 2017. Information and Communication Technologies for Evaluation (ICT4Eval) – Using Innovative Approaches to Development Evaluation. Concept Note. Independent Office of Evaluation of IFAD. Rome: IFAD.

Appendix 1

Evaluation Methodology

This appendix presents methodological fundamentals that are the basis for all IOE evaluations and which, with adaptations, may be useful for evaluations conducted by other evaluation offices or individual evaluators.

Awareness of these methodological fundamentals by evaluators helps to set standards and ensure consistency in methodology and in reporting formats across evaluators and evaluations; it enhances the robustness and rigour of IOE evaluation products and facilitates comparison of results and aggregation. Specific issues and considerations for different types of evaluations are covered in different chapters of IFAD's Evaluation Manual.

IFAD's Evaluation Policy constitutes the overall framework for the independent evaluations conducted by IOE and contains the evaluation principles and operational policies. The key principles are independence, accountability, partnership and learning. According to the Policy, the Manual is a key element for promoting learning and accountability, and 'sets out the methodology and the process that the division will apply in the assessment of the results of IFAD policies, strategies and operations'.[1]

IFAD's Evaluation Policy also states that the IFAD evaluation function shall operate in line with internationally accepted principles for the evaluation of development assistance. IFAD is a specialized agency of the United Nations with a governance structure and operating model similar to that of an international financial institution. As such, IOE subscribes to the overarching norms and standards adopted by the United Nations Evaluation Group (UNEG),[2] ECG[3] and the Organisation for Economic Co-operation and Development (OECD).[4] Consistency and compliance of IOE's work and approaches with these broader principles was at the core of the Peer Review of IFAD's Office of Evaluation and Evaluation Function,[5] conducted in 2009–2010.

These core evaluation principles, which also govern IFAD's evaluative work, are presented in the following box.

Principles for Evaluation of Development Assistance

- Aid agencies should have an evaluation policy with clearly established guidelines, methods and a clear definition of its role and responsibilities and its place in institutional aid structure.
- The evaluation process must be impartial and independent from the process concerned with policymaking, and the delivery and management of development assistance.
- The evaluation process must be as open as possible, with the results made widely available.

For evaluations to be useful, they must be used. Feedback to both policymakers and operational staff is essential.

- Partnership with recipients and donor cooperation in aid evaluation are both essential; they are an important aspect of recipient institution-building and of aid coordination and may reduce administrative burdens on recipients.
- Aid evaluation and its requirements must be an integral part of aid planning from the start. Clear identification of the objectives which an aid activity is to achieve is an essential prerequisite for objective evaluation.

Source: Development Assistance Committee, Paris 1991.

The main purpose of evaluation, according to IFAD's Evaluation Policy, is to promote accountability and learning for better development effectiveness. The range of IOE evaluation products ensures that both these fundamental dimensions of evaluation are adequately covered. Some IOE products (e.g. PCRVs) are strongly oriented towards accountability, whereas others have a greater focus on learning (e.g. evaluation synthesis reports). But the majority of IOE products (e.g. CLEs, CSPEs, impact evaluations and PPEs) cover both accountability and learning dimensions of independent evaluation.

Approach, Design and Methods

IOE evaluations are designed to enable judgement about what has been achieved while also supporting forward-looking operational improvement and strategic guidance at the corporate level. Irrespective of the type of evaluation, the primary purpose of the evaluation drives the design of the evaluation and choice of various evaluation methods. As is pertinently stated in the Evaluation Policy: 'Accountability through evaluation analysis requires a rigorous methodology for the assessment of developmental results and impacts and the performance of the partners concerned.'

In line with the overarching purpose of evaluation in international development cooperation, IOE evaluations follow an objectives-based[6] approach. Such evaluations focus on understanding the pathways to change, the measuring of achievements along the results chain, and generating lessons and recommendations for better performance. The starting point is the broader strategic intent, objectives and design of a policy, strategy or operation, as approved by the Fund's Executive Board, and will examine both the achievement of objectives and unintended results.

IOE also closely follows the international discourse related to theory-based evaluation approaches, as these have advantages over the traditional objectives-based approach. As stated in a World Bank document,[7] 'Theory-based evaluation has similarities to the Log Frame approach but allows a much more in-depth understanding of the workings of a program or activity – the "program theory" or "program logic".' Recommended reading on theory-based approaches can be found in Appendix VI of the Evaluation Manual.

Theory-based approaches will be used in the design of IOE evaluations as and when appropriate. Theory-based approaches will be particularly appropriate, but not limited, to the undertaking of CLEs, especially in those cases when IOE is required to evaluate a policy, strategy or business process for which a specific policy document is not available as a main reference for evaluation. It is also highly relevant for impact evaluations, CSPEs and selected PPEs.

Different methodologies and methods have comparative advantages in addressing particular concerns and needs; and in the end, the question is not whether an evaluation design is ideal, but whether it is adequate given the available budget and capacities and hence 'fit for purpose'. Given constraints and challenges faced, is it able to provide the evidence that makes it possible to pass judgement on what was achieved and explore alternatives? This is also a fundamental principle of the Evaluation Policy: 'IOE shall require the evaluators to ensure that the methods and processes in the Manual are adequately customized – as needed – to reflect the specific circumstances of the policy, strategy or operation being evaluated'. Indeed, a given set of evaluation questions could be answered by a range of different evaluation designs, and different options should be considered, keeping in mind the purpose, context, available resources and budget, and known or anticipated availability of data.

Using a mix of methods – combining the breadth of quantitative methods with the depth of qualitative – and 'triangulating' information from different approaches – can be useful in assessing different facets of complex outcomes or impacts. This will yield greater validity than using one method alone and will usually be the preferred approach in IOE. It is also in line with UNEG good practice: 'A 'mixed method' approach utilizing quantitative, qualitative, participatory and blended (e.g. quantifying qualitative data) approaches is now widely accepted as advisable to address the types of interventions that are now predominant in international development.'[8]

Developing the approach paper is the first step in any evaluation, and a critical one, in which the different methodological options available are considered. The approach paper covers, consistent with IFAD's Evaluation Policy, the following elements: background and rationale; objectives; key questions; methodology and process; time frames; human resources; and communication and dissemination activities. An evaluation framework (i.e. in the form of a matrix) should be developed as the core of the approach paper for each evaluation; the purpose of the evaluation framework is to ensure that evaluators clearly establish the link between the key questions to be addressed, and the data collection instruments and methods, so that a clear evidence trail is established and evidence can be consolidated to support findings. In this respect, evaluators should also observe the implementation modalities of the interventions being evaluated because they may offer opportunities for innovative evaluation designs.

Furthermore, an evaluability assessment[9] should customarily be carried out before the evaluation framework is developed. Evaluability is assessed against the quality and availability of: (i) data deriving from IFAD programme documents available in-house; and (ii) data and information available at the country/programme levels. Special attention will be devoted to the availability of gender-related data and information in all evaluability assessments. The results of the evaluability assessment will allow evaluators to choose the different methods and instruments for collecting data and information to answer the key questions specific to the evaluation framework.

Attribution and Contribution

IOE conducts evaluations with the dual purpose of learning and accountability, but all evaluations also have an element of exploration, aiming to detect to what extent a particular outcome or impact can be attributed to a particular intervention.

This is no easy assessment. First, IFAD-supported activities involve many partners. Second, they are exposed to external factors that influence results; in particular, donor countries' policies, beneficiary countries' domestic policies, other development programmes, socio-economic fluctuations, structural changes and climatic phenomena can affect the results. And third, baselines that may provide strong support for dealing with attribution issues are often not available or not of the required quality. IFAD-supported projects rely on national statistical systems which are generally weak. The database in IFAD's results and impact management system (RIMS) is continually improving, but lack of solid data often remains a constraint to good evaluation.

Therefore, making a credible assessment attributing the results achieved on the ground to a particular project or programme, let alone to IFAD's own performance, is challenging. While this recognition has led to a widespread use of 'contribution analysis' rather than 'attribution' in evaluations, addressing the issue clearly is critical.

Where data allow, two scenarios can be used: the 'before and after' and the 'with – without'. The 'before and after' technique is often hindered by the lack of baseline data and inadequate monitoring and evaluation (M&E) systems, although specific techniques (e.g. memory recall, wealth ranking and community mapping) can shed light on the situation before the project/programme/policy was introduced, thus facilitating the 'before and after' assessment.

The 'with – without' is also referred to as the counterfactual and provides an assessment of impact attribution on an even more comprehensive basis, but is not applicable in all cases. It calls for the definition of a plausible counterfactual, which is the situation or scenario that would hypothetically prevail were there no development intervention. While actual measurement of a counterfactual poses significant challenge and most IFAD projects, even those with a well-functioning M&E system, do not incorporate counterfactual observations (e.g. survey data of households that have not been assisted by a project), evaluators should always apply counterfactual thinking, i.e. ask the question: what would have happened without the intervention?

In cases where data are available, the use of control groups may help to acquire an understanding of the impact of IFAD-supported operations on livelihoods (e.g. in terms of income, nutritional status and access to resources) by assessing the results of interventions on target groups and by comparing them with the situation of populations outside the target group in similarly situated regions. In choosing the beneficiaries and a control group to represent the project population and ascertain project impacts, care should be taken to avoid selection biases. Moreover, evaluators should also reflect at the time of design if there is a likelihood of any systematic errors in measuring impact, and how they will be addressed to ensure greater accuracy in the assessment (see also Chapter 8 of the IFAD Evaluation Manual (2015) on impact evaluations).

In the absence of a control group, alternative methods include general elimination methodology[10] – asking what else may have led to changes – or scenario analysis to estimate the 'without project' situation. While scenario analysis is usually considered a predictive technique, it may also be applied to simulate a counterfactual in retrospective analysis.[11] Also, benchmarking can be used to make a comparative analysis, and the 'causal contribution analysis' approach suggested by Mayne[12] is an approach that has been used in a number of IFAD evaluations.

Notwithstanding the increasing attention to impact, at this stage no consensus has emerged regarding agreed methodologies for rigorously attributing the impact of development interventions to specific factors or causes. On the one hand, some researchers call for a rigorous assessment of causality through quantitative measures of impact and advocate the use of randomized control trials and other experimental and non-experimental approaches (e.g. using propensity score matching methods)[13] as the 'gold standard' of impact evaluation. On the other hand, these approaches have severe limitations in complex and volatile development environments and are skills-intensive and costly, as well as requiring a vast amount of data. Chapter 8 of the IFAD Evaluation Manual (2015) on impact evaluations further analyses the issue of attribution and related methodological fundamentals.

Techniques and Instruments for Data Collection

Data collection tools will vary according to the type of evaluation, availability of data, local context, resources and time available, and other variables. Using a mix of different methods enhances the robustness and hence credibility of an evaluation. Evaluators are encouraged to carefully consider the relevant options to decide on the most cost-effective technique that will provide the most robust evidence for the evaluation. In order to enhance capacity and widen the experience with different techniques in IOE, testing new techniques alongside well-known methods is also encouraged (see Appendix VI of the IFAD Evaluation Manual (2015) for suggested reading on data collection techniques). Approach papers should clarify the rationale for using innovative/experimental methods in the design of a particular evaluation so there is clarity among key stakeholders at the outset of the process.

Specific techniques are required for both data collection and analysis. IFAD's practical guide for M&E at the project level[14] contains a list of 34 different methods, many of which are highly relevant to IOE's evaluations. Table A1.1 highlights some frequently used techniques.

Data can be primary or secondary, qualitative or quantitative, and the evaluability assessment carried out as part of the preparatory process will normally have examined the availability and quality of different types of data. Relevant data for evaluation may be drawn from existing reports compiled by project authorities or IFAD operations staff and from a variety of other sources, including government statistical or administrative offices, national censuses, and world development indicators from the World Bank and United Nations Development Programme. Therefore, during the evaluability assessment, it is important to assess the availability and quality of secondary data. This enables IOE to target efforts towards the collection of additional data. In particular, it is important to ascertain whether baseline data are available and, if so, to determine their quality. Where baseline data do not exist and surveys have not been undertaken or are not of the required quality, the approach paper should identify how data collection ought to proceed in order to secure a plausible proxy for the assessment of initial conditions. In this respect, Internet searches may be useful to identify studies and databases that are relevant for establishing the 'initial conditions'.

To establish baselines, evaluators may conduct in-depth interviews with project beneficiaries and have them reconstruct – using memory recall, structured interviews and/or focus groups discussions – the logical chain of behavioural, productive or organizational changes generated or supported by the project, and the underlying assumptions. Evaluators should exercise caution and triangulate the information secured from diverse sources. This is done before deciding on a set of variables deemed to represent initial conditions and those resulting from project interventions; this is particularly important in the case of income and cost indicators, which may be subject to measurement errors in recall methods.[15]

Case studies are often used in IOE evaluation and present a number of methodological challenges[16] – in particular in terms of validity and generalization. In terms of internal validity, the concern is how to ensure quality, reliability and robustness of methods and design. In terms of generalizations, the concern is external validity, i.e. the extent to which it is possible to generalize, and in which circumstances. And lastly, there are issues relating to aggregation and synthesizing for learning purposes. There is an ongoing international debate on this,[17] and different ways to analyse case study material can be considered, including Qualitative Comparative Analysis, which emphasizes configurations within cases

Table A1.1 The most frequently used data collection methods.

	Typical methods	*Short description*	*Remarks*
Quantitative – structured Qualitative – semi-structured	Direct observations	Observations of sites, practices, living conditions, physical constructions (e.g. grain warehouses) according to a pre-agreed checklist (can be combined with rating).	Necessary in most evaluations; can be a source of unexpected findings. Generalization of findings can be an issue.
	Key informant individual interviews with semi-open questionnaires or checklists	Individual interviews on a number of selected topics according to a pre-agreed checklist. The majority of questions are open-ended and meant to stimulate discussion rather than elicit one-word or one-sentence responses.	Useful for discussing sensitive issues that would not normally be discussed in public. Generalization of findings can be an issue. Requires careful preparation of instruments.
	Focus groups	Interaction of a relatively small group of people (normally 6–12) on a limited set of topics, facilitated by a moderator. Beneficiaries agree on a number of preferences, conclusions, beliefs, attitudes, etc.	Valuable for understanding interactions and areas of dis/agreement. Generalization of findings can be an issue.
	Memory recall	Entails interviews with beneficiaries and other stakeholders, individually or in groups, who reconstruct their situation before the project.	Necessary generally in all evaluations, especially when baseline surveys are not available, but has limitations especially with long recall periods.

Table A1.1. (continued)

	Typical methods	*Short description*	*Remarks*
	Participatory techniques: wealth ranking, problem ranking, community mapping, historical transects	Participants are requested to come up with their own criteria and indicators to assess a situation, a process or a distribution of resources and how it has changed over time.	Indicators and parameters are elicited from people rather than pre-selected by researchers. Generalization of findings can be an issue.
	Case studies	In-depth assessment of a very limited number of observations (e.g. some microfinance organizations, community development projects or farms).	The criteria for the selection of cases are important. Options include selecting best cases, worst cases or a mix of well-, medium- and low-performing cases.
	Large quantitative surveys	These include the collection of primary data from large numbers of beneficiary households and control and comparison groups. Among other issues, such data provide the basis for rigorous assessment – using statistical methods – of the changes in the lives of the rural poor.	Normally done in experimental or non-experimental (project) impact evaluations.

(*Continued*)

Table A1.1. (continued)

	Typical methods	*Short description*	*Remarks*
	Mini-surveys (typically samples of 100–200 respondents, including project and control observations)	A sample of the programme population (and possibly of a control group) is extracted. Interviews are conducted by enumerators on the basis of a pre-written and pre-coded questionnaire. Entries are recorded on electronic support media and analysed using computer software on the basis of standard descriptive, inferential and econometric techniques.	The sampling procedure should try to capture the 'true averages' in the population. This technique is feasible in the context of a project or country strategy and programme evaluation. Trained specialists are required for survey design planning and data analysis.

Note: This table does not provide an exhaustive repertoire of available methods. Evaluation teams are invited to examine the specialized literature.

and uses Boolean algebra to support stronger conclusions from a modest number of cases. Systems modelling that relies on qualitative and quantitative methods and allows existing knowledge to be incorporated into models and then 'run' under different conditions is also an option.

In general there are two main ways to make it easier to draw conclusions and put forward explanations on the basis of relatively few cases: (i) looking at internal relationships within the case as well as comparisons across variables; and (ii) examining the role of theory, whether to test programmes against theory or to develop theories of change during an evaluation.

When primary data collection is necessary, a combination of (mixed) methods should normally be used to ensure data accuracy and facilitate its interpretation. Concerning quantitative data about agricultural production patterns, incomes and livelihoods can be secured through surveys and possibly national statistics, while insights about the performance of development partners may be dealt with through focus group discussions. These may cover issues such as government responsiveness to community needs, availability of privately supplied inputs, or usefulness of IFAD's involvement, all of which help to interpret the data.

Security restraints on mobility, ethical considerations or efficiency concerns may constrain the systematic adoption of random techniques. Nevertheless, there are practical ways to minimize potential biases, for example: (i) selection of project sites so as to cover different agroecological zones; (ii) surveys of beneficiaries at varying distances from a main road to ensure that the direct and indirect impacts on communities are accurately captured; (iii) examination of results in sites where project activities are at different maturity stages; (iv) targeting of communities and organizations endowed with diverse capacities (e.g. a mix of rural credit cooperatives combining high-, moderate- and low-repayment records); (v) interviews of large- and small-scale landholders, sharecroppers and landless labourers; and (vi) surveys focused on older and younger women and men.

A judicious approach should be taken to the sequencing of data collection. For example, when there is more than one mission, interpretation of quantitative survey results secured before the first mission can usefully be checked or probed through participant interviews during subsequent missions. Or, when there is only a single mission, a 'sequential sampling' approach of progressive validation of initial findings can be used.

Analysing and Interpreting Data

The Oxford dictionaries define 'evidence' as the available body of facts or information indicating whether a belief or proposition is true or valid. Keeping quality of evidence at the centre of the evaluation is key to a rigorous and credible evaluation, and the analytical phase is where the strength and validity of evidence is assessed, and any weaknesses of data gaps are addressed. Quality assurance at this stage is essential, and evaluators must ensure that findings are adequately supported by evidence. Reviewers should assess both the quality of the evidence presented and the clarity of the analysis, identifying any possible gaps and weaknesses in the evidence.

Credibly aggregating and synthesizing evaluative evidence poses methodological challenges. Different techniques are used to categorize, clean, systematize, code and analyse data. Some qualitative analysis can be done using simple categorization in an excel format using filter templates for example, followed by synthesis. In other cases, quantitative data need robust statistical analysis, for example to enable a distinction to be made between correlation and causation. Consideration should be given to methods such as the Qualitative Comparative Analysis and other techniques, and the approach paper should indicate the methods foreseen, with the caveat that the data ultimately available may not support these methods and alternatives will therefore have to be found.

> *The quality of evidence is the backbone of a credible evaluation.*

While ensuring that independent evaluations serve as instruments for strengthening accountability, concerted efforts need to be made to understand the proximate causes of good performance or to identify areas of IFAD operations that need further improvement and attention. Hence, evaluation reports should devote adequate coverage and attention to the 'why' question and ensure that the numeric rating attributed to each evaluation criterion is consistent with the evidence secured by the evaluation. In addition to reporting on 'what' the performance was, evaluations should provide a deeper understanding of 'why' the performance was as it was. This in turn facilitates the identification and consolidation of lessons to be considered in country strategy formulation, as well as project design and implementation.

The collection of data and other types of information from different sources and methods[18] – a mixed methods approach – allows the evaluation team to formulate well-founded assessments regarding important dimensions of a project and to triangulate the information and data collected. According to OECD/DAC (Development Assistance Committee), triangulation entails the use of three or more sources or types of information, or types of analysis to verify and substantiate an assessment. This allows evaluators to overcome the bias that comes from single informants, single methods or single observations and thus helps to ensure the robustness and reliability of evaluation findings.

Triangulation in an IFAD project context, for example, could entail looking at the views and perceptions of: (i) project beneficiaries (using, for example, a combination of survey work and participatory techniques); (ii) the country programme manager for the relevant country and/or staff in line departments responsible for project execution (captured using a semi-structured questionnaire); and (iii) secondary sources as documented in project-related self-evaluation reports, such as periodic progress reports, midterm reviews (MTRs) and project completion reports (PCRs). Triangulation can also use other national statistical data, when they are available at a disaggregated level.

Different types of triangulation used in mixed method evaluations

Method	*Examples*
Different conceptual frameworks	Comparing feminist, human rights, social exclusion or economic (e.g. cost-benefit) analysis frameworks
Different methods of data collection	Comparing structured survey, direct observation, secondary data, artefacts
Different interviewees	Comparing interviewee sex, age, ethnicity, economic status, language, etc.
Different times	Comparing responses or observations at different times of day, days of week, times of year
Different locations and contexts	Comparing responses and observations when interviews are conducted in the home when other people are present, in locations where the respondent may be able to speak more freely, in the street and other public places, at work, in the classroom, etc.

Source: Introduction to mixed methods in impact evaluation (No. 3), InterAction, August 2012.

Benchmarking

Benchmarking allows the performance of IFAD to be compared with that of other development organizations. It involves the use of a reference point or standard against which performance or achievements can be assessed.[19] However, there are challenges in benchmarking performance, because no two organizations are exactly the same, and often the evaluation methods and processes used by development organizations may be different.

Notwithstanding the aforementioned, benchmarking is a key aspect in IOE evaluations. Benchmarking performance against IFIs and regional development banks is plausible for IOE, given that IFAD and such organizations have similar operating models (i.e. they provide loans for investments, conduct their own supervision, etc.) and governance structure, and have committed to adopting harmonized evaluation methods as members of the ECG.

Benchmarking is conducted internally with IFAD operations and externally with other relevant institutions. Internally, the results of project evaluations and CSPEs will be benchmarked against the data contained in the ARRI,[20] but also against the data for the specific IFAD geographic region in which the project evaluation or CSPE was undertaken. Benchmarking the performance of IFAD operations across the Fund's five geographic regions will also be a feature in the ARRI.

Evaluations will also – to the extent that this is possible – benchmark results against the indicators and targets contained in the Fund's overarching results measurement framework. Externally, as far as CSPEs are concerned, efforts should be made to collect data and compare IFAD's performance with the results of other IFIs (in particular the World Bank and the appropriate regional development banks) and other international institutions, including the United Nations organizations working in agriculture and rural development, preferably in the same country.

IOE will also use benchmarking as an instrument to learn from the processes or approaches of other development organizations including from United Nations specialized agencies, programmes and funds as well as international non-governmental organizations, and bilateral aid agencies. For example, many such organizations have established country presence for much longer than IFAD, and learning from their experiences and good practices of relevance to IFAD is another form of benchmarking that will be a regular feature of IOE evaluation work, as and when appropriate. Such a form of benchmarking can be particularly useful when IFAD's own experience in a particular development approach or business process might be relatively limited at the time of evaluation.

Evaluation Questions and Inter-Evaluator Variability

The evaluation questions are the point of departure for a robust evaluation. And carefully crafting the evaluation questions is essential to ensure the usefulness and strong ownership of the process.

Evaluation questions are developed at different levels and help focus the evaluation work on a limited number of key issues, thus allowing better reflection on the evaluation criteria, more targeted data collection, more in-depth analysis, and a more useful evaluation overall. Some questions are mandatory in all project and programme evaluations to ensure consistency and comparability. In the absence of questions, choices are likely to be implicit and at risk of being biased; they may be made in relation to the most easily available information, the importance of the various stakeholders, or the evaluation team's preconceptions. Evaluators should ask themselves the question: 'What is it really that we should know?'

A limited set of higher-order questions should guide the evaluation to ensure it fulfils its purposes; these are often generic and linked to specific types of evaluations (impact evaluation, evaluation syntheses, etc.). At the next level, specific questions are tailored to address the issue of focus. Questions should be further unpacked in the form of research questions in the evaluation framework. When evaluations are theory-based, a series of more detailed questions should be developed to inform the TOC analysis. A range of generic questions, including mandatory questions linked to the evaluation criteria should also inform the evaluation, as explained in Appendix II.

> *The most serious mistakes are not being made as a result of wrong answers. The truly dangerous thing is asking the wrong question.'*
>
> *Peter Drucker*

When the evaluation framework builds on an underlying TOC, two types of evaluation questions are relevant: those aiming to uncover 'implementation failure' and those addressing 'theory failure'. The first set of questions addresses questions linked to what was achieved and how well the approach was implemented, understanding why or why not. The focus of the second set is on the underlying theory and its assumptions, and the degree to which these can be confirmed. It answers various questions in relation to how and why, and under what conditions, it worked as it did: knowledge that is essential for scaling-up and replication purposes. In all circumstances, one of the key characteristics of a theory-based evaluation is a solid analysis of the external environment that can generate findings on the influence and implications of external factors for the achievement of results.

The evaluation questions must meet certain criteria. They must first of all be relevant and pertinent. If the evaluation fails to answer key questions for major stakeholders, it will lose relevance and credibility; if it fails to ask the right questions to explore the TOC, it may end up with wrong assumptions and hence irrelevant findings and recommendations; and if it fails to ask mandatory questions that are common to all evaluations of a certain type, it will jeopardize IOE's ability to draw comparisons. Secondly, evaluation questions must be feasible; this relates to the scope of the exercise, the boundaries of the evaluation, and the availability of resources for the evaluation; questions must be commensurate with resources, including time. Getting the evaluation questions right is the necessary basis for any evaluation, and evaluators cannot achieve this alone. Thus, the third criteria relates to the process: questions must be developed using a participatory process to ensure relevance and usefulness for stakeholders, and sufficient time and a strong dialogue process are at the core of the process.

Finally, it is essential that IOE evaluations minimize inter-evaluator variability. The term 'inter-evaluator variability' refers to differences in assessments and judgements related to performance, which primarily stem from differences in the understanding and application of evaluation methodology by IOE staff and consultants. This is a legitimate cause for concern – not only within a given evaluation but also across evaluations – as inter-evaluator variability limits the degree of reliability obtained when aggregating results as well as in comparing results between evaluations.

In addition to providing guidance for the use of numerical ratings, special efforts are being deployed by IOE to minimize such variability, although it should be recognized that it is not possible to completely eliminate this due to the human factor. These efforts include holding a mandatory briefing session for all senior consultants and selected team members on the evaluation methodology and the process to follow; undertaking systematic internal peer reviews within IOE of major deliverables[21] produced during evaluations; requesting each evaluation team member to comment on the ratings and draft final evaluation report; and conducting periodic workshops in IOE to provide guidance to staff and evaluation consultants on the methodologies to be followed and their application. Furthermore, IOE is introducing the use of descriptors to support ratings, which will further strengthen comparability and robustness (Table A2.2).

Theory of Change

Particularly for the theory-based evaluations, understanding the TOC is critical. The TOC may be explicitly stated or, as is often the case, is implicit and therefore needs to be articulate and clarified. A TOC articulates how activities are linked to outcome and impact, clearly outlining the underlying assumptions, including the implicit ones. Assumptions would pertain to external influence, for example, or the assumed behavioural effect of a particular intervention on the target group. The TOC should also capture assumptions about the distributional effects of the interventions in terms of anticipated project benefits to different groups, based on gender, age, geographical location, etc.

The purpose of a TOC is to describe how an intervention leads to results. A TOC illustrates, generally both in graphic and narrative form, the series of assumptions and links underpinning the presumed causal relationships from input to impact; it describes the pathways to change. A TOC also has to factor in the context, something that is often missing in classical logframes, but is essential for understanding when, how, why and under what conditions certain actions lead to certain outcomes, or not, i.e. it is to a very large degree tailored for learning purposes. In this respect, a distinction can be made between programme-level and project-level change. The former would apply, for example, to initiatives aiming at reforms that might facilitate entry into higher value-added areas of production, enhance systemic climate resilience, etc., while the latter might aim, for example, at delivering a set of inputs designed for a beneficiary group of farmers who were not previously using that input. In the former, evaluation tools would need to be able to capture systemic and institutional change, whereas in the latter, the evaluation tools would need to identify uptake, whether beneficiaries understand and trust the technology/input, and whether they have sufficient skill and knowledge.

A TOC may be developed based on past evaluations or theoretical and empirical research on processes of change in similar interventions. It may also be derived from the intervention's existing logical framework; however, it must be developed not merely based on a document describing the logframe, but also based on stakeholder interviews that reveal insights and expectations on the presumed way target groups are affected. In all cases is it important to critically look for, and articulate, plausible explanations for the anticipated changes that can be tested through the evaluation questions and for which evidence may be found.

This said, it should also be kept in mind that use of TOC is a fairly recent phenomenon in IFAD. Therefore, an explicit TOC may not be available in many policies, strategies or operations, and reconstructing the TOC is not always an easy task. In newer projects, it is to be expected that an explicit TOC has been developed, as TOC is not only an evaluation tool, but is also recognized as an excellent tool for stakeholder dialogue in project preparation.

Strong input from stakeholders and beneficiaries is required and therefore the process leading to the articulation of the TOC is important. A robust dialogue with stakeholders will help build ownership, clarify the assumptions, confirm the plausibility of the TOC, and give visibility to those assumptions that are implicit; it can shed light on any discrepancy between what is written in various documents and what is the reality.

> *Getting the TOC right is one of the basic conditions for a good evaluation and therefore sufficient time, effort and resources must be allocated for this.*

This process is time-consuming, may be costly and is not applicable in all cases. Sound judgement should therefore be exercised in determining the necessity and scope of the exercise. In some cases, it is advisable to keep the TOC simple, to use the logframe and make the tacit hypotheses clearer and highlight gaps. However, it should also be noted that as experience is gained, and with systematic sharing of experience and building up a knowledge base, the process will be less time-consuming and the quality of the TOC in IFAD documents may improve.

Much has been written about TOC and how to develop a strong TOC. Appendix VI provides suggested reading and sources on learning, and more details are given in Chapter 8 on impact evaluation, where the construction of a TOC is critical.

Evaluation and Hindsight

There are four evaluation dilemmas that evaluators often need to address:

- How to evaluate performance of a strategy or operation if the context has changed in terms of, for example, the country's policy framework or institutional arrangements?
- How to evaluate performance if development understandings have changed since the beginning of a strategy or operation?
- How to evaluate performance if IFAD policies, processes or features of its operating model have changed during implementation?
- How to evaluate operations whose original targets, approved by the Board as part of design, have changed in the course of implementation?

Common sense might appear to suggest that the evaluation of past performance should be measured by yesterday's metric and the advantages of hindsight disregarded. However, it also stands to reason that results should be judged based on up-to-date information regarding actual achievements and policy standards. Performance cannot be rated as if project and programme designs were immutable and immune to adjustment in the course of implementation. Given the learning dimension of IFAD operations, the adaptability of its instruments and practices should be an important aspect of its performance evaluations. At the same time, revisions of project and programme designs are not cost-free and require the concurrence of partners, in particular the borrowers. Hence, a sound assessment of adjustment feasibility should be carried out by evaluators to ensure fairness in performance ratings.

In other words, in this case learning should be distinguished from accountability. Learning is maximized when it is evaluated against today's standards. But to hold managers accountable for failing to achieve today's standards before they were known may be unfair. For example, to judge the relevance and quality of project designs without reference to the limits of the knowledge available at the time would not be fair. Equally, one cannot expect a rural finance project that is scheduled to close at the end of 2015 to be retrofitted to meet the provisions of a new rural finance policy introduced by the Fund in 2014. In cases where standards or policies have changed late in the life of a project – too late for retrofitting – managerial performance must be evaluated without the benefit of hindsight.

The costs of retrofitting must also be taken into account, for example, in the case of projects or components that cannot be readily changed without prohibitive consequences (e.g. irrigation systems or rural roads). On the other hand, where project and programme designs could have been adjusted economically and in a timely fashion so as to remain relevant as time passed and circumstances changed, performance evaluation with the benefit of hindsight is both legitimate and fair. To sum up, the judicious use of a current evaluative lens[22] allows project performance and impact to be assessed against current standards, and these standards should be clear in the approach paper. This is particularly pertinent in relation to the assessment of IFAD's performance and in this case, evaluation with the benefit of hindsight is important for learning and also for accountability of IFAD's supervision, and should be used to facilitate and encourage adaptation of IFAD's interventions.

Experience shows that the overall development context (e.g. political, agroecological, policy, institutional) in a given country and project area has a significant effect on results. This means that project design teams must factor in context issues up front and that project strategy should be fine-tuned as required during implementation to respond to changes in the implementation environment. Evaluation teams should therefore ascertain the nature of the development context at the design stage, and track its evolution together with adjustments made to the project, including targets, and determine the adequacy, feasibility and rationale of adjustments in the course of implementation, including at the MTR stage. Targets may be changed up until the MTR, provided that the MTR takes place no later than midway through the project. The MTR constitutes the cut-off point for making major adjustments to project/programme targets. Teams are therefore encouraged to ascertain the nature of the development context at the design stage and at the time of the evaluation, as a basis to determine the adequacy of the adjustments made during the course of project implementation. Thus, the benefits of hindsight are used to learn from experience and answer the important question of what could have been done differently in order to maximize results.

Transparency and the Evidence Trail

The credibility and quality of each evaluation are based on the robustness of its evidence and analysis; one consideration in this regard is the importance of ensuring transparency and a clear evidence trail. In terms of transparency, the sources on which findings are based must be clear, and their reliability and validity transparently assessed. Records of interviews should be kept to allow for tracking back to the sources behind a particular finding. The findings and conclusions of a particular evaluation should also be coherently anchored in the analysis and documented in evaluation reports. Each recommendation should find its genesis in the conclusions contained in the evaluation. Moreover, in order to delineate the evidence trail, evaluation reports should contain cross-references to the pertinent sections and paragraphs in the document to help readers easily identify the findings that led to a particular recommendation and the analysis that led to a particular conclusion.

Formulating Recommendations

The above sections focus on how to make evaluations credible and useful. In this regard, the Executive Board noted that IOE should not be expected to make cost-neutral recommendations: it is the role of the Board, together with IFAD Management, to decide on the final trade-off between budget implications and the impact of specific recommendations.[23]

Care must be taken to ensure that recommendations are appropriate for achieving the objectives of the interventions, are positioned strategically, and once implemented, will add value to the organization.

Recommendations must be grounded in solidly evidenced findings and follow logically from the conclusions. It must be possible to track back from a recommendation to the evidence that supports this recommendation and with the transparency described above, be assured that the recommendation is solidly anchored in coherent analysis.

The full utility of an evaluation hinges on dissemination, learning and follow-up and therefore recommendations should be presented in a form that allows different decision-makers to clearly identify their responsibility, and to track follow-up action in IFAD's system for the purpose of the President's Report on the Implementation Status of Evaluation Recommendations and Management Actions (PRISMA) (see also section below). Appendix VI contains a reference to the UNEG good practice note on ensuring appropriate follow-up to evaluations.

Learning Accountability and Follow-Up

Given IFAD's learning mandate, IOE's performance assessment should include an evaluation of the Fund's quality assurance mechanisms, risk management systems, and the adaptability of its instruments and practices. In particular, IOE evaluations should analyse the extent to which recommendations from past evaluations, PCRs, MTRs and supervision and implementation support missions were reflected in the project/programme/policy under consideration. Evaluations should review whether the advice generated through IFAD's quality enhancement and quality assurance processes[24] was internalized in the subsequent phases of project/programme/ strategy/policy development.

Related to this, IOE will undertake evaluations more than once in the same country (e.g. repeat CSPEs in the same countries, after a certain number of years from the previous CSPE) or on the same theme (for example, IOE did a CLE on gender in 2010 and might conduct a similar evaluation on the same topic in the near future). In this regard, such evaluations will specifically entail a careful assessment of how IFAD Management and/or governments (for CSPEs) have acted upon the lessons and recommendations from the previous evaluation(s). A more comprehensive treatment of how evaluation results strengthen the learning feedback loop is included in Chapter 10 on communication, dissemination and learning of the IFAD Evaluation Manual (2015).

As required by the IFAD Evaluation Policy, the PRISMA contains an account of the follow-up actions taken by Management and government (where applicable) on the recommendations made by independent evaluations. It is a key instrument to promote learning and improvement, and is presented each year to the Evaluation Committee and Executive Board together with IOE comments thereon. The PRISMA includes follow-up actions taken to recommendations made in the ARRI, CLEs, CSPEs, PPEs and evaluation synthesis reports. The PRISMA also includes an account of how IOE comments on the Report on IFAD's Development Effectiveness have been treated by Management.

For the ARRI, this includes recommendations agreed with the Board. For CSPEs, these are extracted from agreements at completion point finalized at the end of the evaluation. For CLEs and evaluation synthesis reports, these are outlined in Management's responses or action plans submitted to and agreed by the Executive Board following evaluations. As far as PPEs are concerned, the PRISMA only includes the recommendations addressed to IFAD Management.

In terms of process, after the evaluations are selected, recommendations are extracted, listed and classified by selected themes for follow-up. The list is prepared by the Programme Management Department (PMD) Front Office and reviewed by IOE. The classification criteria used include level (country, project etc.), nature (operational, strategic, policy) and theme.[25]

Joint Evaluations

Joint evaluations[26] can contribute to progress towards implementation of the provisions contained in the Paris Declaration which are aimed at promoting aid effectiveness and can help overcome attribution problems in assessing the effectiveness of programmes and strategies, the complementarity of partners' contributions, the quality of aid coordination, etc. Of course, there are various degrees of 'jointness', depending on the extent to which individual partners cooperate in the evaluation process, merge their evaluation resources and combine their evaluation reporting.

Joint evaluations permit the pooling of resources to undertake more effective desk and country fieldwork that will almost certainly add to the coverage, quality and credibility of the evaluation. They also provide an opportunity to draw together the substantial volume of evaluative evidence, experience and knowledge accumulated by more than one organization. Properly managed, they may also help reduce transactions costs, which the country or countries covered by the evaluation must assume. On the other hand, joint evaluations are more demanding than single-owner studies because there is increased scope for disagreement on methods, priorities, findings or resource management and because of sensitivities about reputational risk. Similarly, the coordination of joint work has often proven complex and has increased the cost and duration of the evaluation exercise as a result of the coordination costs incurred in terms of staff time and travel, lengthy management processes and other factors.[27]

In view of changes to the aid architecture and stronger evaluation capacity in some countries, and the increasing use of partnership approaches, evaluation on a broader scale than the traditional project, sector or thematic levels is likely to be required, not only to assess results at the country level but also to look more closely at the role of the different institutions in the process. Joint or multi-aid agency evaluations can provide this broader perspective while fostering cross-agency learning and reducing evaluation transaction costs for in-country stakeholders; there may thus be a shifting of transaction costs from the partner country to IFAD, which is well in line with the Paris Declaration and IFAD's commitment to partnerships.

IOE will carefully consider joint evaluations and participate selectively in them, including with the Rome-based agencies, with which such evaluations have already been carried out. IOE will continue to contribute to the ongoing debate on joint evaluations taking place within the framework of UNEG, ECG and the DAC Network on Development Evaluation.

Participation

The DAC Quality Standards for Development Evaluation[28] contains a standard related to stakeholder engagement: 'Relevant stakeholders are involved early on in the evaluation process and given the opportunity to contribute to evaluation design, including by identifying issues to be addressed and evaluation questions to be answered.' Research in turn suggests that this seems to enhance the use of evaluation findings and that learning and the use of findings are stronger when the link between users and producers of knowledge is short. This is reinforced through one of the basic tenets of IFAD's Evaluation Policy, namely 'partnership' as the policy states that IOE's procedures and instruments aim at the appropriate engagement of partners in the evaluation process while safeguarding the independent role of IOE.

Involving beneficiaries is particularly important, including at the design stage where they may bring a different perspective from policymakers. Involving beneficiaries in the early stages may broaden the focus of the evaluation, but is also perceived to enhance fairness and provide for a more balanced evaluation, and programme stakeholders are often aware of contextual considerations of which evaluators are not. Therefore, by including stakeholders in the evaluation process, the evaluation is more likely to identify important problems of concern[29] and hence ultimately enhance credibility and utility.

IOE evaluations will pay due attention to promoting participation of key stakeholders in the evaluation process, but at the same time ensure that the independence of the evaluation's analysis and final judgements are not compromised. Key stakeholders who IOE will seek to involve – at different stages of an evaluation, which will vary depending on the type of evaluation being conducted – include IFAD Management and staff, recipient governments, cofinanciers, and ultimately beneficiaries and their organizations.

Participation will be promoted in several ways. For example, key stakeholders will be given an opportunity to provide inputs at an early stage of an evaluation so that their concerns and priorities are captured (e.g. in the form of key questions) in the design of the evaluation. Evaluations will ensure that different stakeholders may interact with IOE at selected junctures, so that they may share their experiences, data and information to facilitate an informed evaluation. They will also be given a chance to comment on the draft final report, and IOE will carefully consider their feedback before finalizing it, with due consideration to the independence of IOE. Beneficiaries would also be involved at other stages of the evaluation, for example, at the time when final workshops are held at the country level by IOE to discuss the main conclusions and recommendations from CSPEs.

Evaluation Management

Managing an evaluation involves agreeing on how decisions will be made for each cluster of the evaluation (from designing an evaluation to reporting and supporting use) and ensuring they are implemented well. Three aspects are particularly important: transparency, ownership and maximizing learning.

To demonstrate transparency, evaluation processes and methodology should be discussed with key evaluation partners,[30] while evaluation reports should include data and information that adequately support the conclusions as well as relevant descriptions of the evaluation process, the literature consulted and the working papers generated to support report findings and recommendations. The entire evaluation report and supporting working papers are disclosed together with the approach paper.

In accordance with the IFAD Evaluation Policy, the designated IOE lead evaluator will be responsible for the quality and contents of the final evaluation report. In line with this Policy, IOE staff lead the evaluation with the required technical inputs from consultants. IOE will make efforts to mobilize national consultants, especially for project evaluations and CSPEs, and ensure they satisfy all necessary provisions in IOE's conflict of interest policy (see Appendix IV of the IFAD Evaluation Manual [2015]) for consultants. Efforts will also be made to ensure gender balance of evaluation teams.

With regard to learning, much informal learning actually takes place during the evaluation process as evaluators engage with stakeholders and beneficiaries and ask questions, often giving rise to new insights and ways of seeing and appreciating things. Formal learning is more embedded in 'uptake chains' and good feedback loops; this requires that lessons learned are absorbed in a systematic, structured and effective way into policy and practice. This is further explored in Chapter 10 of the IFAD Evaluation Manual (2015) on communication, dissemination and learning.

Notes

1 www.ifad.org/gbdocs/eb/102/e/EB-2011-102-R-7-Rev-1.pdf, para. 26 (v).
2 www.uneval.org/document/foundation-documents.
3 www.ecgnet.org/document/ecg-big-book-good-practice-standards.
4 www.oecd.org/development/evaluation/dcdndep/41612905.pdf.
5 www.ifad.org/gbdocs/eb/ec/e/62/e/EC-2010-62-W-P-2.pdf.
6 www.ecgnet.org/document/good-practice-standards-evaluation-public-sector-operations.
7 World Bank: *Monitoring and Evaluation, Some Tools, Methods and Approaches*, 2004.
8 www.unevaluation.org/document/detail/1433.
9 For guidance on conducting evaluability assessments see: www.gov.uk/government/uploads/system/uploads/attachment_data/file/248656/wp40-planning-eval-assessments.pdf.
10 First introduced by Michael John Scriven, this requires the listing of plausible alternative causes.
11 See ADB, *Strengthening the Quality of Project Economic Analysis in ADB Operations*, Manila: ADB, 2008, pp. 7–8.
12 Mayne, J. (1999) *Addressing Attribution Through Contribution Analysis: Using Performance Measures Sensibly*, Mimeo, Office of the Auditor General of Canada, Canada, and www.innonet.org/resources/node/437.
13 Propensity score matching methods are often used to control for bias when randomization is not possible. These methods were developed to ensure comparability between the treatment and the comparison group in terms of propensity to participate in the development programme. The first step involves estimating the likelihood (the propensity score) that a person/household would have received the treatment or intervention given certain characteristics. After estimating the propensity scores, the scores are used to group observations that are close to each other. Comparisons of development results can then be applied to different groups of observations which have the same propensity to participate, hence ensuring comparability (see Ravallion, M., 1999. The Mystery of the Vanishing Benefits: Ms. Speedy Analyst's Introduction to Evaluation. Working Paper No. 2153. Washington, DC, World Bank).
14 See Appendix D in A Guide for Project M&E (2002).
15 Typical problems with recall methods include: (i) incorrect recollection; and (ii) telescoping, i.e. projecting an event backward or forward. For example, the

purchase of a durable good which took place seven years ago (before the project started) might be projected to a point in time just four years ago, during project implementation.

16 See for example www.gao.gov/special.pubs/10_1_9.pdf.

17 For a thorough review, see papers prepared for the International Workshop: Case studies in Development Evaluation, Validity. Generalization and Learning, Copenhagen 2012. www.um.dk/en/danida-en/results/eval/reference-documents/workshp12/.

18 See A. Tashakkori and C. Teddlie (1998), *Mixed Methodology: Combining Qualitative and Quantitative Approaches.*

19 See Glossary of Key Terms in Evaluation and Results-Based Management, OECD/DAC.

20 The ARRI is produced every year and contains the aggregate performance assessment of all evaluations conducted in a given year. It normally covers all five IFAD geographic regions.

21 Mainly the evaluation approach paper and the draft final report.

22 Evaluation approach papers should clarify instances when a current evaluative lens will be applied to assess a specific policy or operation.

23 See minutes of the December 2014 Executive Board: www.webapps.ifad.org/members/eb/113/docs/EB-113.pdf.

24 These are new processes introduced under IFAD's Action Plan to improve quality at entry. The quality enhancement process is the responsibility of PMD, whereas the quality assurance process is undertaken at arm's length from PMD under the responsibility of the Office of the Vice-President.

25 Currently categorized in six broad categories: targeting and gender; technical areas; project management; non-lending activities; cross-cutting themes; and corporate issues, mainly information and communication technology and human resources issues.

26 IOE worked on a major joint evaluation with the African Development Bank on agriculture and rural development in Africa in 2007-2008. A section on the joint evaluation is found in the IOE website on the IFAD portal (www.ifad.org/evaluation).

27 For a more comprehensive discussion of these matters, see *Guidance for Managing Joint Evaluations*, DAC Evaluation Series, OECD, Paris, 2006.

28 www.oecd.org/development/evaluation/qualitystandards.pdf.

29 See A.E. Cullen, C.L.S. Coryn and J. Rugh: *The Politics and Consequences of Including Stakeholders in International Development Evaluation.* American Journal of Evaluation, 2011.

30 Key partners may include, for example, IFAD Management, government authorities and project staff who are the main users of evaluation results.

Appendix 2

Evaluation Criteria, Key Questions and Ratings

Background. In line with good practice in international development evaluation, IOE uses a set of evaluation criteria to assess the performance of IFAD policies, strategies, operations and business processes. In the different types of evaluations it undertakes, IOE rates (i.e. scores) performance across each criterion using a six-point rating scale. It also has two specific evaluation criteria – project performance and overall project achievement – that provide an integrated assessment of performance of IFAD interventions.

Evaluation criteria applied in IOE evaluations ensure the harmonization of IFAD's evaluation methodology across international development organizations. The evaluation criteria adopted are in line with the practices set out in the OECD/DAC Glossary of Key Terms in Evaluation and Results-Based Management,[1] the UNEG's Norms and Standards, as well as ECG's Good Practice Standards for the Evaluation of Public Sector Operations. Taken together, these criteria allow a solid assessment of the key aspects of IFAD initiatives to be made, and also enable comparison with peers who apply similar criteria to judging performance.

IOE has introduced additional evaluation criteria[2] which allow it to assess key dimensions that are specific to IFAD's work and operating model. The criteria used, their definitions and the rating system will be discussed later in this appendix.

To help conduct performance assessments and ensure consistency in the foundation for ratings, IOE uses a number of core questions for each evaluation criterion. These core questions have been carefully crafted, based on the internationally recognized definition of each evaluation criterion. The core questions are therefore fundamental and evaluators should aim to provide answers to all of them and assign a rating to each evaluation criterion. The answers to each question should be clearly outlined in each evaluation report. Additional evidence for each question should be available, possibly in a synthetized form, in the documentation retained on the evaluation for transparency purposes, but does not have to be presented in the report. The use of core questions will help ensure consistency and comparability as well as allow for aggregation of ratings across IOE evaluations.

In addition to core questions, evaluators may also introduce other questions for each criterion, to ensure a comprehensive assessment of the intervention being evaluated. Additional questions are meant to deepen the inquiry and provide further evidence to support the finding and assessment. The approach papers, prepared at the outset of each evaluation, should specify the criteria, how they are applied, and the questions for assessing each criterion.

Evaluation criteria and their definitions. The evaluation criteria used by IOE and their definitions are given in Chapter 2 of this book, under the 'evaluation criteria' sub-section.

Evaluation questions by criteria. This section provides an overview of the core questions to be addressed by each evaluation criterion used by IOE.

Rural poverty impact. Given the international emphasis on measuring impact of aid interventions and IFAD's commitment to a significant poverty impact, building up a strong database with evidence on impact is indispensable. IOE applies a specific criterion to gauge rural poverty impact, which should be treated with the utmost thoroughness. The criterion will be rated to enable comparisons and tracking of trends over time. The following are the core questions all evaluations should try to answer in assessing rural poverty impact:

Has the initiative had the anticipated impact on the target group?[3]

To what extent have beneficiary incomes changed as a result of the project?

In what way have household net assets changed due to the intervention?

What changes have taken place in household food security and nutrition and what explains such changes?

In addition, and in light of IFAD's mandate, there are four impact domains in areas of priority for rural transformation promoted by IFAD: (i) household incomes and assets; (ii) human and social capital and empowerment; (iii) food security and agricultural productivity; and (iv) institutions and policies. Covering the four domains is not mandatory in every evaluation, and the performance of operations in any of these areas is not to be rated. The evaluation approach papers should clarify which domains will be covered and why.

Project performance. This is a composite criterion made up of four core performance criteria: relevance, effectiveness, efficiency, and sustainability of benefits. They are mandatory and are always applied and rated in CSPEs and project evaluations. Where an exception is made, the reason must be made clear in the approach paper and the final evaluation report. Each of these four criteria will be assessed and rated individually. Evaluations will determine overall project performance by taking an average of the four individual ratings for relevance, effectiveness, efficiency, and sustainability of benefits.

The two criteria, effectiveness and impact, while distinct, are closely linked. The effectiveness criterion assesses whether the intervention has met (or is expected to meet) its objectives. By contrast, the rural poverty impact criterion takes on board all effects, intended or unintended, direct or indirect, positive or negative, and thus requires careful examination if it is to be used to shed light on IFAD's role as an agent of rural change. The risk of duplication when assessing these is mitigated by focusing the effectiveness criterion on the achievement of the immediate outcomes of the project and on the initial effects, whereas all side effects and longer-term effects are captured by the impact criterion. The use of these criteria thus leads to a deeper understanding of the forward and backward linkages of an IFAD-funded operation. As a result, they help guide efforts to scale up such operations and to orient the design of future IFAD projects.

Sustainability of benefits. This is a multi-dimensional concept as acknowledged in Occasional paper 8: Sustainability of Rural Development Projects (IFAD, 2009), and merits careful assessment. In line with the OECD/DAC definition, sustainability entails two aspects: (i) measuring whether the benefits of an activity are likely to continue after donor funding has been withdrawn; and (ii) assessing if benefits are environmentally as well as financially sustainable, i.e. the likelihood that actual and anticipated results will be resilient to risks beyond the project's life. (Environmental aspects are explored separately under the criterion environment and natural resource management.) This criterion should be assessed in all IOE evaluations. Country strategy and programme and project evaluations should include a rating for this criterion.

Below are the core questions for assessing and rating relevance, effectiveness, efficiency, and sustainability of benefits.

- **Relevance:** (i) Are project objectives in line with key IFAD and government objectives for promoting sustainable agriculture development as well as the needs of the rural poor? (ii) Was project design appropriate (for example, in terms of components, financial allocations, institutional arrangements, etc.) to meet the intervention's objectives? (iii) Was the project adjusted during implementation to any changes in context to retain continued relevance?
- **Effectiveness:** (i) To what extent have the objectives of the project and its components been attained in quantitative and in qualitative terms? (ii) In particular, what changes in the overall context (e.g. policy framework, political situation, institutional set-up, economic shocks, civil unrest) have affected or are likely to affect project implementation and overall results? (iii) What factors in project design and implementation account for the estimated results in terms of effectiveness; are there valid alternatives?
- **Efficiency:** (i) How does the economic rate of return at evaluation compare with that at project design?[4] (ii) What are the loan costs per beneficiary (both at the time of appraisal and at the time of evaluation) and how do they compare to other IFAD-funded operations (or those of other donors) in the same country and/or other countries? (iii) What are the total project management costs in relation to total project costs and how do they compare with similar projects?
- **Sustainability of benefits:** (i) Do project activities benefit from the engagement, participation and ownership of local communities, grassroots organizations and the rural poor, and are adopted approaches technically viable? (ii) Is there a clear indication of government commitment after the loan closing date, for example, in terms of provision of funds for selected activities, human resources availability, continuity of pro-poor policies and participatory development approaches, and institutional support?

(iii) What are the chances that benefits generated by the project will continue after project closure and what is the likely resilience of economic activities to post-project risks?

Gender equality and women's empowerment (GEWE). This criterion is also assessed in all evaluations by IOE, and therefore country strategy and programme and project evaluations must include a rating for this criterion. A dedicated section in all evaluation reports provides an overall assessment of IFAD's efforts in promoting GEWE. Each evaluation assesses performance based on the main objectives outlined in the relevant country strategies and project design, and the 2012 corporate gender policy[5] or any revisions to the policy in the future.[6] Evaluations will also assess IFAD's efforts to integrate the main provisions in the handbook issued by the UNEG on human rights and gender equality.[7]

The following are the core questions that evaluations must cover to assess efforts made to promote GEWE:

- What were the project's achievements in terms of promoting GEWE? This includes assessing whether there are changes: to women's access to resources, assets and services; to women's influence in decision-making; in workload distribution among household members; in women's health, skills, income and nutritional levels; in gender relations within households, groups and communities in the project area; etc.
- What percentage of total project resources was invested in activities to promote GEWE and how does that compare with other projects funded by IFAD?
- To what extent did the project define and monitor sex-disaggregated results to ensure that GEWE objectives were being met?
- Was the project implementation structure adequate to support effective implementation of GEWE goals?

Innovation and scaling up. IFAD devotes priority attention to promoting pro-poor innovation and scaling up of successful innovative approaches introduced in the context of IFAD operations. The IFAD Evaluation Manual (2015) indicates that evaluators should give only one final consolidated rating for both innovation and scaling up, and that the criteria should be considered equally in the analysis, narrative and judgement. However, in 2017, IOE and IFAD Management (represented by PMD and SKD) prepared a revised agreement to harmonize the Fund's self-evaluation and independent evaluation systems by assessing innovation and scaling up separately and providing a separate rating for each criteria. Therefore, starting with the evaluations conducted in 2017, IOE has been rating innovation separately from scaling up.

Innovation. The assessment of innovation is to be based on the IFAD Innovation Strategy[8] or further enhancements thereof over time, as well as findings and recommendations from the CLE on innovation and scaling up.[9]

The core questions below should be answered by evaluators in assessing innovation.

(i) What are the characteristics of innovation(s) promoted by the intervention? (ii) Are the innovations consistent with the IFAD definition of this concept? (iii) Are the actions in question truly innovative or are they well-established elsewhere but new to the country or project area? (iv) Have grants been used to promote innovation?

Scaling up. The assessment of scaling up is to be based also on the IFAD Innovation Strategy, the findings and recommendations from the CLE on innovation and scaling up, and the dedicated document presented to the Tenth Replenishment Consultation in 2014 on Scaling Up Results.[10]

Evaluations will consider IFAD's 'operational framework for scaling up results' (2015), in particular by paying attention to whether design and implementation paid due attention to the 'pathways, drivers, and spaces' for scaling up results of IFAD operations. The operational framework notes that: (i) the definition adopted by IFAD for scaling up is 'expanding, adapting and supporting successful policies, programmes and knowledge so that they can leverage resources and partners to deliver larger results for a greater number of rural poor in a sustainable way'; and (ii) scaling up results does not mean transforming small IFAD projects into larger projects. Instead, IFAD interventions will focus on how successful local initiatives will sustainably leverage policy changes, additional resources and learning to bring the results to scale.

The core questions below should be answered by evaluators in assessing scaling up.

- **Scaling up**: (i) What evidence was used to justify scaling up, and were successfully promoted innovations documented and shared to facilitate scaling up? (ii) Has IFAD proactively engaged in partnership-building and policy dialogue to facilitate the uptake of successful innovations? (iii) Based on the information available, have these innovations been scaled up and, if so, by whom? If not, what are the prospects at the time of evaluation that they can and will be scaled up by the government, other donors and/or the private sector? What were/are the pathways to scaling up?

Environment and natural resource management. This criterion should also be assessed in all evaluations by IOE.[11] Country strategy and programme and project evaluations should include a rating for this criterion. A dedicated section in all evaluation reports would provide an overall assessment of IFAD's efforts in environment and natural resource management. Each evaluation would assess performance based on the main objectives outlined in the relevant country strategies and project design and IFAD's environment and natural resource management policy.[12]

The following are the core questions that evaluations would cover:

- To what extent did the project adopt approaches/measures for restoration or sustainable management of natural resources (e.g. enhancement of ecosystem services, support to training and extension to foster efficient environment and natural resource management, uptake of appropriate/new technologies)?

- To what extent did the project develop the capacity of community groups and institutions to manage environmental risks (e.g. how governance-related factors are shaping the management of natural resources, influence of incentives and disincentives for sustainable natural resource use and natural resource-based livelihoods improvement)?
- To what extent did the project contribute to reducing the environmental vulnerability of the community and build resilience for sustainable natural resource management that contributes to poverty reduction (e.g. factors such as access to technologies, information/awareness creation)?
- To what extent did the project contribute to long-term environmental and social sustainability (e.g. through avoiding over-exploitation of natural resources or loss of biodiversity or reduction of the community's livelihoods); by empowering and strengthening the capacity of community-based natural resource management groups to ensure sustainable natural resources management; and by ensuring strong stakeholder engagement, especially of vulnerable groups, in decision-making affecting natural resources use?
- To what extent did the project follow required environmental and social risk assessment procedures (e.g. Social, Environmental and Climate Assessment Procedures), including meaningful consultation with affected and vulnerable communities, and comply with applicable IFAD or national environmental and social standards or norms, to ensure any harmful impacts are avoided or managed/mitigated through, where needed, the implementation of effective environmental and social management plans, including robust monitoring and supervision?

Adaptation to climate change. The contribution of the project to increase climate resilience and increase beneficiaries' capacity to manage short- and long-term climate risks will be assessed in all evaluations by IOE contingent on the adequacy of evaluative evidence. This dimension has only recently become an IFAD priority; hence older projects may not have addressed this and little evidence will exist. Country programme and project evaluations will include a rating and a dedicated section in all evaluation reports will provide an overall assessment of IFAD's efforts. Each evaluation should assess performance based on the main objectives outlined in the relevant country strategies and project design and IFAD's Climate Change Strategy.[13]

The following are the core questions that evaluations will cover:

- To what extent did the project demonstrate awareness and analysis of current and future climate risks?
- What are the amounts and what is the nature of funds allocated to adaptation to climate change-related risks?
- What were the most important factors that helped the rural poor to restore the natural resource and environment base that (may) have been affected by climate change?

Performance of partners: The performance of each partner – IFAD and government – is examined and reported on separately, as each has specific functions and roles to discharge. All country programme and project evaluations should assess and attribute a rating to the performance of IFAD and the government.

With regard to the performance of the relevant government, it is important to note that IOE assesses the performance of government in the agriculture sector, with specific reference to IFAD operations. IOE evaluations do not aim to assess government performance in general terms.

Moreover, it is noted that different government ministries, departments and line agencies (at the national, provincial and local levels) may be involved in project execution. As such, evaluations will need to make an assessment of the individual institutions involved and, ultimately, come up with a comprehensive overall rating for the performance of the government concerned. In light of the sensitivities involved, special attention should be devoted to discussing the assessment and ratings of government performance with the main government agencies involved and to seeking, on a joint basis, ways and means to enhance government performance in the future, as may be required.

The following are the core questions to be covered in assessing and rating IFAD and government performance, respectively.

- **IFAD:** (i) How well were the comments and recommendations of quality enhancement and quality assurance processes, including from evaluations, included in the final project design? (ii) Did IFAD have a well-functioning self-evaluation system? In particular was adequate supervision and implementation support provided and a MTR undertaken in a timely manner, and portfolio performance monitored on a continuous basis? (iii) Did IFAD exercise its developmental and fiduciary responsibilities adequately, ensuring that projects had sound financial management systems, audit reports were submitted in a timely manner, the required provisions in the financing agreements were fully met, etc.? (iv) What support did the IFAD country office (where applicable) provide to the country programme and individual operations? (v) Did IFAD pay adequate attention to further cooperation and dialogue with the United Nations Rome-based agencies?
- **Government:** (i) Did the government ensure that a baseline survey was done in a timely manner and that M&E systems were properly established and functioning? (ii) How were periodic progress reports used and was the PCR provided in a timely manner and of the required quality? (iii) Were counterpart resources (funds and staffing) provided in line with the agreement at design stage? (iv) Were audit reports done and submitted as needed? (v) Was the flow of funds and procurement procedures suitable for ensuring timely implementation? (vi) Did government have the required capacity at all levels to implement the project as per schedule?

The section below clarifies the use of evaluation criteria by different types of IOE evaluations.

CLEs: These are the most complex and challenging evaluations done by IOE, covering various types of IFAD policies, strategies, operations and business processes. Therefore, depending on the nature and scope of the evaluation, the specific evaluation criteria used will be defined in the approach paper, as drawn from the criteria shown in Table A2.2. There may be instances when additional criteria, not included in this chapter, are also used in certain CLEs.

CSPE: These evaluations will be based on three inter-related components to be assessed: (i) portfolio-level analysis of IFAD-funded projects included in the CSPE scope; (ii) non-lending activities – policy dialogue, knowledge management, partnership-building; and (iii) the performance of partners (i.e. IFAD and the government) in managing the country programme, including process aspects.

Based on the composite assessment of these three components, CSPEs will provide an aggregate rating for the IFAD-government partnership in promoting rural transformation. The evaluation criteria, their definitions and key questions are described in Chapter 6 of the IFAD Evaluation Manual, on the methodology and process for CSPEs.

With regard to the assessment of the project portfolio, each project included will be assessed and rated for the following criteria: relevance, effectiveness, efficiency and sustainability of benefits, project performance (as an average of the four aforementioned criteria), rural poverty impact, GEWE, innovation and scaling up, environment and natural resources management, and adaptation of smallholders to climate change, as well as IFAD's performance, and government's performance as a partner. If a criterion is not applied in a particular CSPE, the reasons for this should be explicitly stated in the approach paper.

Based on these ratings – excluding IFAD's and government's performance – an overall project portfolio achievement rating will also be determined. However, it should be noted that for ongoing projects assessed as part of CSPEs, it might not be possible to assess and rate all the criteria. This is because some ongoing projects might have been under implementation for only a short while at the time of the CSPE, and therefore it was not possible to assess their performance across all evaluation criteria adopted by IOE (e.g. in terms of effectiveness or impact). The criteria to be assessed in depth will be set out in the approach paper for CSPEs.

Each non-lending activity will be rated for relevance and effectiveness, but only one rating is to be provided for policy dialogue, knowledge management

Table A2.1 Rating system.

Score	*Assessment*	*Category*
6	Highly satisfactory	SATISFACTORY
5	Satisfactory	
4	Moderately satisfactory	
3	Moderately unsatisfactory	UNSATISFACTORY
2	Unsatisfactory	
1	Highly unsatisfactory	

Table A2.2 Score descriptors.

Rating scale	*Score descriptor*
Highly satisfactory (6)	Under the concerned criterion, the activity (project, programme, non-lending, etc.) achieved or surpassed all main targets, objectives, expectations, results or impacts, and could be considered as a model within its project typology.
Satisfactory (5)	Under the concerned criterion, the activity achieved almost all (indicatively, over 80–95%) of the main targets, objectives, expectations, results or impacts.
Moderately satisfactory (4)	Under the concerned criterion, the activity achieved the majority (indicatively, 60–80%) of the targets, objectives, expectations, results or impacts. However, a significant part of these was not achieved.
Moderately unsatisfactory (3)	Under the concerned criterion, the activity did not achieve its main targets, (indicatively, less than 60%) objectives, expectations, results or impacts.
Unsatisfactory (2)	Under the concerned criterion, the activity achieved only a minority of its targets, objectives, expectations, results or impacts.
Highly unsatisfactory (1)	Under the concerned criterion, the activity achieved almost none of its targets, objectives, expectations, results or impacts.

and partnership-building. Based on these three individual ratings, CSPEs will also generate a composite rating for non-lending activities.

Project evaluations and validations: PCRVs, PPEs and impact evaluations. These evaluations are done for completed operations, and therefore will cover all evaluation criteria to be rated as shown in Table A2.2. There might be instances when not all evaluation criteria can be assessed or rated. For example, IOE might not be able to assess or rate 'adaptation to climate change' in a project that mainly deals with microfinance for micro-enterprise development, or projects that were designed a decade ago that did not explicitly emphasize climate change. In such cases, the evaluation report will allocate a 'not applicable' rating to such criteria.

Evaluation synthesis reports. These IOE knowledge products primarily focus on summarizing lessons learned, and good or less good practices. The analysis in a synthesis report will include a review of four evaluation criteria: relevance, effectiveness, efficiency and sustainability of benefits. However, these criteria will not be rated. The approach paper for an evaluation synthesis report will clarify if any other criteria is to be covered, together with the rationale for doing so.

The rating system. Starting in 2005, in line with the practice adopted in many other IFIs and United Nations organizations, IOE moved from a four-point to a six-point rating system[14] that allows for a more nuanced assessment of project results.

In addition to reporting on performance based on the six-point rating scale, in 2007 IOE introduced the broad categories of 'satisfactory' and 'unsatisfactory' for reporting on performance across the various evaluation criteria (see Table A2.1).[15]

As a general rule, evaluators will exercise their own judgement in assigning ratings, supporting their arguments with evidence. In this regard and based on the evidence available, evaluators are encouraged to make full use of all the points on the rating scale, rather than merely being satisfied with assigning ratings in the middle of the range. It is essential that the narrative on findings is consistent with the rating assigned. All ratings (except project performance) will be a round number, with no decimal points. Consistent with most other evaluation offices (except the Asian Development Bank) and to keep the system simple, no weights will be assigned to ratings when determining a final rating for project performance or overall project achievement. Evaluators are encouraged to consult the detailed score descriptors of the PCR guidelines. In addition, IOE has developed guidance to support evaluators to assign ratings on each evaluation criteron (see Table A2.2).

Notes

1 www.oecd.org/development/evaluation/2754804.pdf.
2 Innovation and scaling up, GEWE, and environment and natural resource management and climate change.
3 This entails trying to determine and report the total approximate number of people (gender disaggregated) who have been affected by the initiative being evaluated.
4 To be assessed only where adequate evidence exists, and using the following internal guidelines: www.xdesk.ifad.org/sites/pt/FAME/EFA/Economic%20%20Fiancial%20Analysis%20Documents/Guidelines/EFA_guidelines_Aug2013.pdf. (This is an internal link).
5 www.ifad.org/gender/policy/gender_e.pdf.
6 A gender marker system was developed by PTA Gender Desk in 2014 to provide a uniform method to assess the gender sensitivity of IFAD projects at various stages of the project cycle. See www.slideshare.net/GenderSecretariat/ifad-gender-markers.
7 See document 'Integrating Human Rights and Gender Equality in Evaluation (2012). The document can be found on the following website: www.uneval.org/document/detail/980.
8 www.ifad.org/gbdocs/eb/91/e/EB-2007-91-R-3-Rev-1.pdf.
9 www.ifad.org/evaluation/public_html/eksyst/doc/corporate/scalingup.pdf.
10 www.webapps.ifad.org/members/repl/10/3/docs/IFAD10-3-R-2.pdf.
11 For projects and programmes pre-dating IFAD's environment and natural resource management policy, this is optional and contingent on sufficient evaluative evidence.
12 IFAD (2012) Environment and Natural Resource Management Policy.
13 www.ifad.org/climate/strategy/e.pdf.
14 Where 6 is the highest score and 1 the lowest score.
15 The Annual Review of Development Effectiveness produced by the Independent Evaluation Group of the World Bank uses a similar system of categorization.

Index

Page numbers in italics refer to tables.

2030 Agenda *see* Agenda 2030

accountability 16
adaptive management 33
AfDB–IFAD Joint Evaluation 66–67
African Development Bank (AfDB) 4, 14, 66, 132n26
African Evaluation Association 97
Agenda 2030 1, 61, 69, 85, 100
agreement at completion points (ACPs) 10–11, 50, 51n14
agricultural statistics 103
American Evaluation Association 97
Annual Report on Results and Impact of IFAD Operations (ARRI) 47–48, 121, 128, 132n20
Asian Development Bank 4, 14
Australasian Evaluation Society 97

Bangladesh 45
benchmarking 121–122

Caribbean Development Bank 4
children 71–73
China 86–87, 98–99
climate change *27*, 138
Collect Earth data collection tool 105
community-based organizations (CBOs) 72–73
completion evaluations 36
conflict-affected states/situations 61–64
Consultative Group on International Agricultural Research (CGIAR) 96
corporate-level evaluations (CLEs) 46, 55–66, 140
country programme evaluations (CPEs) 13, 19, *22*, 42, 45, 46
country strategic opportunities programmes (COSOPs) 33, 35, 42, 43–44, 51n14, 86
country strategy and programme evaluations (CSPEs) *22*, 33, 42–44, 51n14, 121, 140

data analysis and interpretation 119–121
data collection 114–119; *see also* mobile-based data collection tools
decentralization 64–66
direct supervision 56–57
Drucker, Peter 122

Ecuador 43
efficiency 59–61
environmental sustainability *27*, 85–86, 137–138
Ethiopia 71
European Bank for Reconstruction and Development 14
European Evaluation Society 97
evaluation *see* independent evaluation
evaluation capacity 9, 98–99
Evaluation Committee (IFAD) 11, 17, 19–20
Evaluation Cooperation Group (ECG) 12, 13–15, 96, 104, 121
evaluation criteria 21, *22*, *25–27*, 32, 133–142

evaluation management 130–131
evaluation methodology 20–35, 110–131
evaluation questions 122–123
evaluation ratings *see* rating scales/systems
evaluation syntheses 46–47
evidence 119
External Review of the Results and Impact of IFAD Operations (2002) 53–55

field presence 57
focus groups 89
focused evaluations 36
follow-up actions 128
Food and Agriculture Organization (FAO) 4, 80, 81–82, 96
Fu, Haishan 106

Garcia, Oscar A. 106
gender equality and women's empowerment (GEWE) *26*, 55, 57–58, 62, 69–79, 136
gender marker system 142n6
Global Environment Facility 4
Guatemala 71
Gulf War (1991) 45

harmonization agreements 31–35
Heider, Caroline 105
HIV/AIDS 66
Hui people (China) 86

impact evaluations 41–42, 141; *see also* rural poverty impact
independent evaluation 9–50
Independent External Evaluation of IFAD (IEE) 54–55
Independent Office of Evaluation of IFAD (IOE) xi–xii, 6: evaluation products 36–50; influential evaluations 53–67; peer reviews 13–15; relationship with Executive Board and Evaluation Committee 17–20
India 71
indigenous peoples 79
Indonesia 71
information and communication technologies (ICTs) 103–106
innovation *26*, 55–56, 136–137
Inter-American Development Bank 4, 14
inter-evaluator variability 123–124
interim evaluations 36
International Development Evaluation Association 97–98
international financial institutions (IFIs) 2, 11
International Fund for Agricultural Development (IFAD): establishment 2–3; governance 3–4; UN partners 4; *see also* Independent Office of Evaluation
International Telecommunication Union 103

joint evaluations 128–129

Kenya 65
Khadka, Shyam 92

Latin America and the Caribbean Network for Monitoring, Evaluation and Systematization 98
Lavizzari, Luciano 11
learning 89–95, 127–128; *see also* past performance

Malhotra, Ram 9
Mauritania 45
methodology *see* evaluation methodology
microenterprise interventions 78
mid-term evaluations 36
mid-term reviews (MTRs) 126
Millennium Development Goals (MDGs) 100, 109n4
mobile-based data collection tools 105
Mongolia 81

natural resource management *see* environmental sustainability
Nepal 71, 72, 73

OECD/DAC (OECD/Development Assistance Committee) 32, 120
Organisation for Economic Co-operation and Development (OECD) 3–4, 19, 110
Organization of the Petroleum Exporting Countries (OPEC) 4

Papua New Guinea (PNG) 71, 72–73
Paris Declaration 128
partner performance *27*, 139
past performance 125–127
pastoralists 80–82
performance-based allocation systems (PBASs) 4
Philippines 93–95
President's Report on the Implementation Status of Evaluation Recommendations and Management Actions (PRISMA) 35, 89–92, 128
primary data collection 119
private-sector entities 107
project completion report validations (PCRVs) 13, 32, 34, 35, 38, 39–40, 141
project performance *26*, 134–135
project performance evaluations (PPEs) 13, 32, 34, 35, 38, 39, 40, 141
propensity score matching methods 131n13

qualitative comparative analysis 115, 120

Rapid External Assessment of IFAD (1994) 9–10
rating scales/systems 21–24, 32, 141
recommendations 127
Rice, Theresa 92
Rome-based agencies 96, 102–103, 106
rural poverty impact *25*, 134
Rwanda 43, 77–79

scaling-up *27*, 56, 136, 137
Segone, Marco 105
self-evaluation 31–35
Shanghai International Program for Development Evaluation Training 99
Spitz, Pierre 44
stakeholder engagement 129–130
Sudan 45
sustainability of benefits *26*, 135–136
sustainable development 85–88
Sustainable Development Goals (SDGs) 1, 85, 100–103, 107
Swedish Agency for Development Evaluation 92
Swiss Agency for Development Cooperation 98

Tanzania 54
thematic studies 36
theory of change (TOC) 27–31, 74, 122–123, 124–125
transparency 127, 130
triangulation 120–121

United Nations 4
United Nations Evaluation Group (UNEG) 97, 104, 110

water conservation and management 87–88
Wilton Park (UK) 99
women *see* gender equality and women's empowerment
World Bank 4, 14, 45, 71, 112
World Food Programme (WFP) 4, 96
World Wide Web 103

Xi Jinping 87

Yemen 45
youth interventions 82–84

For Product Safety Concerns and Information please contact our EU representative GPSR@taylorandfrancis.com Taylor & Francis Verlag GmbH, Kaufingerstraße 24, 80331 München, Germany